I Still Believe

I Still Believe

mental illness and suicide
in light of the Christian faith

Desiree Woodland

Desiree 2011

Library of Congress Control Number:		2011900739
ISBN:	Hardcover	978-1-4568-5357-0
	Softcover	978-1-4568-5356-3
	Ebook	978-1-4568-5358-7

This book was printed in the United States of America.

To order additional copies of this book, contact:
Xlibris Corporation
1-888-795-4274
www.Xlibris.com
Orders@Xlibris.com
89120

Table of Contents

Dedication

This book is dedicated to my friends and family, especially my husband Gary and daughter Michelle. It is through the blessing of relationship that we are able to process the sorrows of life. And it is through those relationships we receive the strength of love and faith in God to move forward and make our lives count for others.

Epigraph

"Mental illness is so common that if even a small proportion of the patients made a special effort to learn as much as they could about their illness, and if they proceeded to educate their families and friends, there would not be too many uninformed people left and the stigma associated with mental illness would be virtually eradicated."

Dr. John Varsamis,
Society for Depression and Manic Depression of Manitoba
Newsletter, April 1990

*A mother's story about her son and the mental illness
that changed him,
his subsequent suicide and what
Christian faith means in the light of it all.*

Desiree Woodland

Foreword

2 Corinthians 6:10 " . . . as sorrowful, yet always rejoicing . . ."

"Matt, you have to go your sister Desiree's house right now," my wife Renee's voice quaked. "Renee, what's wrong? What happened?" She choked out the words, "Your nephew Ryan took his life." I ended the call and began the drive to her house on Indian Farm Lane; it was the longest twenty minute drive of my life.

The violent death of my nephew Ryan brought unimaginable grief to the Woodland family. Though time has changed the intensity of their grief, it is clear that in this lifetime it will linger. Yet, in the midst of Desiree's sorrow there has been and there remains joy. And by *joy* I don't mean the absence of sadness, or tears, or groaning. I don't mean some type of cheap, frivolous, *praise God anyhow* type of cheerfulness that betrays reality. This joy is hard to describe but I believe you will see glimpses of it in this book. The title, "I Still Believe," perhaps says it best. When people are chest deep in the temporal blessings that this life offers and say, "God is good," I don't think this impresses anyone. But when people suffer unbearable loss, when they are severely afflicted and still they say, "God is good, He remains my hope, I still believe," it makes God look precious—more precious than all that we love in this world. My sister has made God look more precious in my sight.

In this quote from the *Screwtape Letters* by C. S. Lewis we hear the voice of the devilish imp Screwtape speaking about God and man's relationship to Him in suffering, "He wants them to learn to walk and must therefore take away His hand, and if only the will to walk is really there He is pleased even with their stumbles. Do not be deceived Wormwood. Our cause is never more in danger, than when a human, no longer desiring, but intending, to do our Enemy's will, looks round upon a universe from which every trace of Him seems to have vanished, and asks why he has been forsaken, and still obeys."

If you are someone who has experienced deep and painful loss and are wondering how it is possible to keep on, keeping on when we live in a broken world, full of broken people, when you feel broken yourself and feel like you don't have any resources left for anybody, then I trust that the story of my sister Desiree's journey will be a blessing to you. By the way—it can be done. It seems impossible, but by the grace of God, it is possible to be a person who weeps with those who weep and yet possess unshakable joy. My "big sister" is a living example of this paradox.

Matthew Ellison
President of 1615 Ministries
Albuquerque, New Mexico

Preface

After Ryan's death I was hungry for what the past would reveal to me about my son. I pored over old journals where I found a Scripture I had prayed for him in 1995. *I will not be afraid of evil tidings, my heart is fixed trusting, leaning on and being confident in the Lord.* Psalms 112: 7. When I read it once again, I fell down in a puddle of tears because I *was* afraid. I had always prayed for my children and prayed daily for Ryan after his diagnosis; prayed for freedom in his thinking, his hearing, his life, and for a complete cessation of the pain of his ears—essentially for a healing. My prayer was not answered in the way I wanted and I questioned God's purpose in allowing this to happen to Ryan, to our family.

As humans, the question of God's existence and/or His goodness haunts us after a tragedy of life-changing proportions. It became of the utmost importance that I settle the constant attacks in my mind about the goodness of God. I felt compelled to continue on in the walk of faith and reason that I began so long ago, despite deep doubts that had arisen. I had come to faith in Jesus at age fourteen and been a regular part of the church for over thirty years. Being a Christian had shaped my life; I had known no other way to live. Until now, I had not understood the significance and importance of Christians as thinking people who ponder hard ethical questions about life and death and then search for answers. I had always had a pat answer ready for any trial. But when the mysteries of death seemed to yield none, rather than giving up on belief, I reached out into the blackness of night to grab hold of Someone bigger than myself.

Chapter One

SUICIDE

When a person says or thinks 'I don't want to live anymore' he may actually be saying I am weary of dying every day. It is not life I am tired of, but death.

The day Ryan died, Monday May 1, 2006, began like a million other days. Getting ready for work, having coffee, reading my Bible, saying my prayers, and saying goodbye to my family were my regular routine. Since our daughter Michelle had left home many years before—and our son had moved back in, the household consisted of me, my husband Gary and Ryan. Lately, a brief feeling of foreboding came over me each time I said goodbye to Ryan. There was an almost palpable sense of impending doom about the way he was not getting better. But summer vacation would be coming, and for a teacher, a bit more time to devote to life outside the classroom, so I made a mental note that I would talk to his doctor then. We mumbled our goodbyes as usual and as I rushed out the door, I wondered what Ryan would find to occupy his time.

Soon, my mind filled with thoughts of the day's lessons. Teaching was rewarding, but demanded my full attention. So, after a busy day with students, I couldn't wait to get to the gym for my work out. It was my way of unwinding before making dinner and grading papers. When I got home I threw my schoolbooks on the chair and sank into the couch. Bailey, one of our two dogs ran over and sat on my lap. I don't remember if he seemed overly anxious or not. I noticed the phone blinking with a message—it was my husband asking me to call him at the hospital. His mom had gone for surgery earlier that day, but was still in the operating room six hours later. "Don't come to visit yet," he explained. "They'll call us when she gets out." I immediately went to tell Ryan of the change of plans because he had agreed the day before to go with me to visit his grandmother in the hospital.

Walking outside towards the self-contained room we had recently built for him, I thought of our outing the day before. Surprisingly, he had offered to join me and my 6th grade class at a park for some hands-on medieval activities with the Society for Creative Anachronism. The society engages in activities that demonstrate life in the Middle Ages. I was delighted because since his diagnosis he had retreated into almost constant seclusion. It was rare that he went anywhere that might be too loud for his ears. He had been acting strangely since he became convinced he was losing his hearing.

I remembered arriving at the park where my students, filled with excitement, raced up to my car. "Mrs. Woodland, is this your son?" and then questions for Ryan tumbled out of their mouths. "How old are you?", "Do you skateboard?" He nodded and the faintest hint of a smile crossed his face. I felt happy. Maybe this outing was a sign that he was going to get better. Maybe he would start interacting with the world again. I hoped.

I had given him a quick hug as we got out of the car, just before a sweet girl from my third period class grabbed my hand and pulled me towards a group dance lesson where people in medieval costume were ready to begin. "Ryan, would you like to join us?" He shook his head and said he'd just go sit down by one of the giant cottonwoods and take it in from a distance. Satisfied, I continued towards the melodic sounds of flutes and drums.

In my mind's eye I still see him as he wandered across the park where another group of students were testing their abilities as knights. Dull metal swords clanked against hard leather shields. I remember being surprised that Ryan wanted to be so close to that kind of noise. But, no matter, it was a gift. I had no idea that it was the gift of spending his last day with me.

Rounding the corner to his room, I was shocked out of my reverie. What was wrong with Ryan? No, this cannot be. Primal sounds I did not recognize came from some deep place within me. I couldn't catch my breath, my throat caught and I couldn't seem to keep down the bitter taste of some dark unknown emotion, and yet I could not stop the sounds. Uncertain of what lay before me, my body quivered with raw fear. My mind rebelled—fighting to understand, my brain told me he had fallen. Is that a pipe? Maybe he fell on the pipe. Maybe that's how he got the hole in his head. No, I don't want to see this. This cannot be. But, there he was. Ryan stretched out on the threshold of his room, not moving. What to do? Call 911, or call Gary . . . 911 busy, Oh God! What do I do? Take his pulse again—surely HE CAN'T BE DEAD! Nauseating waves of anguish threatened to strangle me as I frantically ran from his room, to the front yard, to the kitchen, unable to take in reality.

I could only see the upper part of him because he lay on the threshold and I could not enter his room. I am sure this saved me from the sickening results of a gun exploding at close range. Nothing seemed real; it could not be Ryan lying there, nor was I standing over him in this surreal slice of time. Not wanting to believe, but somehow knowing it was true. He was gone.

"Oh, my God, Gary, it's Ryan, I think he's dead. Ryan's dead." I barely heard his confused reply, "What did you say?" I screamed again, "Ryan is dead, Ryan is dead." I repeated the same mangled conversation when I called my daughter and then my dad. This awful thing had to be a mistake. In recent months he had told me many times that he would never kill himself, so I allowed myself to pretend that any moment he would wake up. "Please wake up, Ryan." I stared at my beautiful child's crumpled form lifeless on the ground.

Within minutes of those phone calls neighbors and friends appeared at the door, questioning why an ambulance was in front of our house. They must have let themselves in because I was only aware that darkness had enveloped me and that the air that had become thick and suffocating.

"It was the illness," my friend who understood mental illness boldly spoke to me through the numb reality. Seconds later my husband, parents, sisters and brother arrived. I hugged them all screaming, "Oh my God, oh my God, over and over." It was a blur of medical examiners and paramedics. I told them, "He left us a note; I know he left us a note. Did you find the note?"

I watched as they wheeled his lifeless body out to the emergency vehicle with the clothes on his back, his wallet in his pants pocket, and the shattered glasses still on his face. They found a blue covered notebook with Ryan's easily identifiable handwriting, but with words I did not want to accept.

I held the precious book that contained his last words and kissed it, clutching it to my heart willing him to come back. I tried to read the words which had been written with a steady, not erratic hand, but I could not. My brother, Matthew, continued reading. I listened to words that seemed too well thought out, too planned, too intentional.

"I am Ryan Woodland. Born June 2, 1981. An artist, musician, mechanic, wanna'be engineer, car and stereo fanatic, thinker, skater, son, brother, and friend whose pants were always hanging just a little too low. I want you all to know that I am, that I was, a once vital, living, breathing, and creating human being . . . someone with an identity and dignity, who wanted only to live normally again. Please forgive me. And never forget that I love you all so much. I loved being your son and brother. I know we will all see each other again someday."

How could I believe these words? Tears blinded me as I struggled to read it once more. "We will need to take that notebook as evidence." I looked into the paramedic's caring eyes. *Evidence of what? It was obvious what had taken place. But why? Why had he done this unspeakable thing?*

So they took him away; took his last words away, and left us with nothing but a phone number to reach the office of the medical examiner so we could get his personal effects returned. As part of the investigation, the officer asked us a hard question. Did we want to donate Ryan's organs? "The questionnaire is long and painful," she warned. "Someone from the Organ Donation program will call tonight." Within minutes the phone rang.

"I am sorry for your loss. It is a brave and selfless thing for you to do, and the questions will be painful. Please try your best to complete the interview. OK, number one: If the heart is useable do you want it to be donated? Number two: What about tissue? Must it be used to save or support a life, or can it be used for cosmetic surgery?" The ragged-edged words cut deep, "No, cosmetic surgery is out. Ryan's organs must be used to save or support life only." After twenty grueling minutes Gary hung up the phone. His voice sounded small and lost, "I got so choked up, Des, I didn't know if I could finish."

Gary's lips trembled. His face, no longer able to conceal the shock of grief, was haggard and tired. He looked older somehow, different. Death does that. Just hours before he hadn't known what the Office of the Medical Examiner did, and now he and his family were inextricably linked. Nothing would ever be the same.

Sleep did not come that night.

Early the next morning, as consciousness slowly seeped into my brain, the misery and depression were so thick I could scarcely breathe. Death hung like a heavy curtain. It lurked in the corners of the house; it guarded the doorways so I could not escape, for I was now living in a world without my son. O God . . . without my son. *Why would I want to continue living?*

I forced myself out of bed, for what I didn't know. *Why would I want to continue living?* Nothing had meaning. If this horrible thing could happen in my world, then life had no meaning. In spite of the lives that I held dear, my husband, my daughter, my parents, I couldn't think past the moment. And in this moment I wanted to die in order to relieve the heavy weight of my heart. Somehow the idea brought a bizarre comfort. I rebelled against this life without Ryan.

Ryan had been my *best boy* all his life, even as he approached young manhood. He loved to tease me about growing old and pretended to see white hairs growing on my chin. In spite of the ravages of his illness, when we were together his laugh had been cheerful and full of mischief. How would I live without the sound of his laughter?

My body was burdened with sorrow, and the sense of hopelessness grew heavier with each step downstairs—stairs Ryan would no longer climb. Gary walked behind me. "This isn't real. It can't be real," he said. "It's a nightmare from which we're never going to wake." I nodded, staring at nothing.

Trying to piece together some answers I forced myself to think about the events leading up to his death. Several years before, Ryan had complained of an impending deterioration in his hearing, but it had never shown up in audiograms. Still, he was insistent that it was real. Yes, this belief had been odd, and it had changed him, but we didn't worry excessively about it. It was not serious in our minds. My husband Gary, daughter Michelle and I just got used to not understanding this behavior.

"Ryan, your friends have been calling. They asked you to call back. Won't you please? I think it would do you good to be with them,"I pleaded. "Mom, why would anyone want to hang out with me, when all I can talk about is my hearing and balance problem?" "Ryan, I know you feel there is something physically wrong with you, but tests haven't confirmed this. Couldn't you just go and get your mind off this problem?"

This was our form of communication lately. No, he would not go anywhere that might further damage his ears. This "something" had affected his plans for the future as well as his social and personal life with his family. We were at a loss of what more we could do to help him; much less to identify the "something" that was stealing him away.

Erroneously, we thought he might gain a sense of independence and self esteem to live on his own, and maybe this would make a difference. After all, he was twenty four. So we helped him move into a studio apartment. This was the beginning of the end.

He was never at peace there. Living alone was too terrifying and his mind created a frightening scenario out of a simple accident. He jumped over a block wall and cut his leg. The deep cut probably required stitches, but he never told anyone about it.

After one application of Neosporin to the cut, all of his thoughts focused on the perceived total destruction of his hearing as a result. He checked online and read about the damage that could result from too much Neosporin. Never mind, that when he called local doctors they assured him that he would have had to ingest tubes of the stuff for such damage to occur. He could think of nothing else but trying to heal his ears, anyway. I had never seen behaviors like these—wringing his hands, pacing, talking irrationally about driving to Mexico and driving off a cliff. He couldn't be still. Up, down, talking to himself, sighing deeply. His high state of anxiety was frightening. Seeking a friend's advice, I immediately took him for a psychological evaluation. We got lost on the way and had to circle around the block several times before we found the office. I remember trying to comfort him. *We will find out what's wrong. Ryan, it will be ok.*

I was lost that day in August 2005, nine months before he died, the day we were thrust into the institutional world of mental illness. I am not a psychiatrist, nor a psychologist, nor a social worker. I knew there were changes in my son, but I had not known these changes were symptoms of mental illness.

And so we entered the psychologist's office unsure of what lay ahead. With a brief introduction, she invited him into her private office and shut the door. I sat alone in the waiting room, thumbing through magazines, but mostly praying, for what seemed like an eternity. He came out several times to test his hearing with his homemade equipment, which he had brought along in an old shoebox. Ryan had tried to restore his perceived hearing loss by building a laser with parts obtained from Germany which were not available in the U.S. He had been using this laser daily, but today, he directed this dangerously high intensity laser at his ears every five minutes, then used a home audiogram trying to detect a change.

He tried to take the laser with him into her office, but she asked him to leave it with me. Something seemed to be controlling him and he was *compelled* to check his ears. She watched helplessly and I sobbed as he completed another test. He handed the shoebox back to me, the box that contained the tools of his delusion. Head phones attached to a black box with a red flashing light. He wore the panic and anguish on his face and he no longer looked like Ryan.

All our worries had become fear in these several months leading to today. When the evaluation was finished, the door opened and she asked me to come in. Her eyes gave away the seriousness of his condition. I sat down next to Ryan; I could hardly bear to see him in such pain. And I could hardly bear to hear her words, "He is in the middle of a psychotic break and needs to be hospitalized." Her voice was sad, but firm. Ryan didn't object, he just wanted some relief from the overwhelming anxiety, and agreed to go for an emergency psychological evaluation.

This compulsive behavior was shocking to witness, but must have been pure terror for Ryan. Very afraid for him, I witnessed this mysterious, irrational behavior take over my precious son. My helplessness was magnified and it overwhelmed me. Thankfully Ryan was admitted to the psychiatric hospital. He had no insurance and thus became another person with a mental illness dependent on the mercy of the state.

After a stay of only three days, I naively thought he was on the road to recovery. He was prescribed standard psychiatric medications— antipsychotics, anti-anxieties, and antidepressants. I trusted that the medication was a vital part of his healing. Since his symptoms were so severe, it made sense to use such powerful ones. But the medical model of treatment is only one piece of a plan. Therapy, the other piece, attempts to retrain a brain that cannot perceive reality. Ryan was never able to engage in this kind of therapy because the level of his delusion was not lessened or alleviated by any of the medications.

Ryan's Journal

"I can't pretend that I'm ok anymore. I'm devastated and I don't want to live anymore—not like this. It's constant torture 24 hours a day. I'm sorry if you think it's all in my head because it's not. The antibiotic—it did all of this—it ruined my life. I cannot stand one more day of this. I'm sorry it had to be this way: I love all of you. I will see you again, someday. BTW, when I say 'this' I mean the ringing, the hearing loss, I can't relax. It's driven me to kill myself. I'm so sorry everyone. I really am. I love you all so much. I'll be at peace. No more pain. No more pain. No more pain. I want to live, but not like this. This is hell to me. The only reason I have been trying so hard to be normal again is for you guys. I know how much it hurts you to see me nonfunctional, so I tried for as long as I could. I so much wanted to be normal again, but it just couldn't happen. Every day I looked at normal people like I used to be and I'd just break down. I can't be the person I was because I'm in so much torture every day. It will never be the way it was."

Emotional pain was the theme of his days and nights. Every conscious thought throbbed with the belief that he was going deaf. His perceived loss was becoming a burden that he could no longer bear. He didn't understand, either, why this was so important to him. The audiograms would never show what he knew was true. He *knew* he was going deaf and he *believed* that he started the deterioration by listening to loud music years before.

But it was the application of Neosporin that preceded the psychotic break. He believed it was killing hair cells in his ears. So to Ryan, the talk of going to Mexico made sense because he *had* to get the antidote for the Neosporin. It was the final factor, in a series of things over the course of years that he believed were robbing him of his hearing, and it pushed him over the edge. In addition he found people on the Internet who had lost their hearing and committed suicide. Did this provide him with the faulty logic to do something so drastic?

For the first two weeks after Ryan died, I told his story over and over in graphic detail to all who entered our home. Each retelling was excruciating but it was a way to digest the reality and force it into each crack and crevice of my brain. Silence is an enemy not to be tolerated after the death of a loved one by suicide. A Harvard Mental Health Letter sent by a friend says, "Suicide is more painful for the family than other kinds of death and harder to acknowledge. The survivors often suffer from guilt and shame that prevent normal mourning." The specter of suicide cast its shadow over everything.

Each morning, with my first glimmer of consciousness, guilt was there too with its suffocating diatribe. Each evening as I tried to fall asleep I saw his lifeless body and would try to envision his last minutes over and over. I relived the trauma of finding him in daytime flashbacks, seeing his body drained of spirit, lying crumpled on the threshold. The sheer power of this emotional rollercoaster threatened to undo me. I was in disbelief, and kept pretending that he would be coming home soon. Numbness spread through me until the force of reality overpowered me and I fell over, a helpless mess. No, he was not coming back. Overtaken by confusion and exhaustion, I just wandered from room to room, looking for something, sensing I had lost something. Then I remembered; I would not find him. Ryan wasn't coming home.

Eventually I would come to learn this was a normal response after a violent death. Each retelling hammered into my body, mind and soul, the truth that Ryan was gone. The sharp edge of reality cut deeper with each passing day. But, it was the sharp edge from each retelling that allowed me to compare the reality and the fantasy concerning each detail of Ryan's death.

It was so unfair, and the sadness of his last days made it more so. This was not supposed to happen. Life was not supposed to turn out like this. *What hadn't I seen? What hadn't I understood?*

Day after day came the excruciating realization—*I am still here.* Pain coursed through me every hour, every minute. I reached out to the psychologist who first saw Ryan, since it was she who recognized the psychosis and had named what was happening to him. I trusted that I could once again rely upon her for support.

My husband and I also began attending the local Survivors of Suicide support group. I hadn't known a group like this existed. It's a group in which no one wants to be a member. No statement could ring more true.

We survivors met in a church fellowship hall. A propped open door led to a dark lobby. The sunlight couldn't squeeze through the thickly paned windows, so the only light was from the open door. Mechanically, Gary and I moved forward down a hallway that seemed to have no end. I recall how our shoes squeaked on its freshly polished floor, announcing the arrival of the newest members. I remember a lump in my throat that I could not swallow and the sting in my eyes from staring at that floor. Or was it from the tears?

There was a person at the end of the hall who greeted us and asked our names. Such information seemed inconsequential and unimportant. It hurt to even mumble our names. Someone else directed us to empty seats and pushed a tissue box near to us. The room was filled with the tortured anguish of the newly bereaved—we were all living in a nightmare, except that it was real. Going around the circle we told the name of our loved one, how they died and how long ago. I barely whispered Ryan's name, and trembled as I screamed, *he shot himself three weeks ago.* Once again, I didn't recognize the sound of my own voice. My body convulsed with sobs, but no one stopped me. Handing me the tissues, they listened. They had been here before. Gary and I didn't spare any of the details. It was a blessed relief to share this unbearable 'thing' that had happened and was too overwhelming for ourselves alone. We heard of death by hanging, asphyxiation, pill overdoses, and guns.

At first other's stories only reflected our pain. We were so consumed with our own grief that we could see only Ryan's suffering. It seemed odd, because we have always supported others in pain, but now we could not. No one else's suffering seemed to equal our own. In grief one becomes self-absorbed and suicide added another layer to complicate the grief process. Telling it over and over through the ensuing weeks and months helped us frame our thinking around this awful thing that had now become a part of our lives. We had a need to tell Ryan's story.

It took a long time and attendance at many meetings before we could genuinely listen to others' stories. Each time though, it became easier to open ourselves to the pain of others. Survivors with the most time between them and the death had gained perspective. Their grief, not fresh, left us with a tinge of hope that we maybe we also could heal in time. *But did I want to heal? Give me my grief. Give me my son.*

Wanting my son so desperately, I remember the intense nightmarish agony of my dreams. I could sense the heavy, dead weight of my own flesh, the blood pulsing through my veins and the sheer desolation that imprisoned my mind and kept me from my son. This body of flesh is after all only the tent that houses the spirit. A paradox! It is precisely in this life and body of flesh that we are to glorify God and show forth His power. I awoke with a start immediately aware of the throbbing pain of my heart.

I was inescapably confronted with Ryan's perspective that the constraints and limitations of his own earthly shell were too confining. He could not see the beauty of the world anymore. The searing pain in my heart lingered throughout the day.

Ryan's Journal

"Let me start by saying that I am going deaf. This is something I accidentally brought on myself. There is nothing any doctor or I can do about it. To me hearing = life. All the subtle sounds, enjoying a loud party, hearing all your friends joking behind you, listening to your family say "I love you," and vice versa, hearing yourself say it to them. This is certainly the reason I became drawn at an early age to electronic audio equipment, and to music. The sounds were spectacular and I had the best sound system I could afford. As an insecure child, music brought me out of myself, allowed me to connect with others in a way I had never imagined. Just sharing a new found song or CD could form strong friendships. I have no doubt that music affects people on a level no other art form or media can. It is a God-given and appointed gift. Without it, the world would be in a much sorrier state than it currently is. I'm trying to explain my situation to the best of my ability, so you guys won't wonder why. But I don't think any explanation will really make it ok. I'm so sorry you guys."

My life's focus became a quest for understanding what Ryan went through. I began to read books on mental illness and suicide, and then shared them among my new circle of friends. Our lives had all been shattered because of a child's suicide and all of us were searching for answers that may never be found, but we searched anyway. We had to.

In a book called *Andrew, You Died Too Soon*, Corrine Chilstrom tells her story, and like me, she wrote and studied to help heal. Faith was a support, as was education about the clinical aspects of suicide. Quoting Edwin Schneidman from *The Definition of Suicide*, there are six distinct categories of suicides—reasons why someone would take his or her own life. Each suffers a particular kind of pain: *1) rational: to escape pain, 2) reaction: following loss, 3) vengeful: to punish someone, 4) manipulative: to thwart someone's plan, 5) psychotic: to fulfill a delusion, and 6) accidental; reconsidered too late.*

Did Ryan fit into one of these neat and tidy descriptions? Yes, he wanted to escape the pain of constant worry and thoughts about his ears and yes, he had the delusion that he was going deaf, and he fulfilled it. But, still there seemed to be pieces missing. This answer seemed too simple, too neat and tidy. The human mind is so complex and what is known of mental illness is conflicted and often confusing. Could I recreate the story of his illness, filling in the missing pieces from what I learned so that I might begin to understand?

For nine months he grew and was nurtured in my womb. Filling the air with words of love and hope, I had spoken to my unborn son, hoping they crossed the barrier between us. And for the nine months following his diagnosis, despite the medications, the psychotic/ delusional state continued to grow and develop in Ryan's psyche, and my words of love could not penetrate his reality. The delusion took him prisoner and he experienced the physical sensations of deafness because his brain convinced him it was so. Not that it could have been fixed. Mental illness cannot be fixed. It is much more complex than just taking a pill and being cured. There is a series of depressions, anxieties that can be precursors to a full blown severe illness like schizophrenia. Ryan had been given several different diagnoses. Schizophrenia? Delusional disorder with depression? Diagnosis is based on observable criteria, and it is not always clear which characteristics fit into which category of illness since they overlap. Knowing so little about mental illness then, and not realizing the ramifications of such kinds of diagnoses, we still believed he would be all right.

Which of Ryan's symptoms indicated mental illness? All I knew was he didn't fit in the world anymore; years earlier he had already started to believe he was going deaf. There were subtle changes, which we attributed to growing pains. But his life had begun to slowly and silently unravel. In the dark recesses of his being, hidden from view, there was an illness lying dormant that would choke out the promise of who he might have become. In his last two years the struggle became outwardly visible as he isolated himself and was consumed with a hearing loss that was not there. Perhaps I had thought his preoccupation would just magically disappear. But, he didn't fit in a world that required him to be a certain way, to do a certain job, to interact with others. I had glossed over my worries about how he was struggling to find his place. But, Ryan's sister Michelle had given up trying to have a relationship with him. His last year of high school she made a real effort to get him to go out and visit friends. She had wanted to introduce him to her girl friends who had asked to meet him, or she invited him to just go to the movies. He always had some excuse as to why he couldn't and it revolved around his hearing. "No", he said, "I'll just stay home and hang out. I have stuff to do, anyway." After a while it became too tedious to try.

On rare occasions he would join Gary and me for dinner as long as the restaurant was quiet. So, we routinely ate at the same restaurants just to take him with us. We made excuses because of love and tried to accept his way of being in the world. We accepted that he was not able to go to college, that he was no longer a social being, and that he was preoccupied with his hearing. But, instead of seeing these behaviors as signals that something was terribly wrong, we allowed him to change and loved him in spite of them. If we had seen them as warning signs would early treatment have made a difference? I wrestle with this thought as it rips my heart afresh.

I wanted to give him the benefit of the doubt and to support him; I listened as he spilled out his sadness over the perceived loss. The final audiologist's report from 2005 stated, "Essentially normal hearing with no evidence of pathology." I tried to appeal to his reason by restating the results, but this proved futile. "It doesn't matter what the tests show, I know it's real," he would say.

"Ok, say you do have hearing loss, can't you please just let go of it and get on with life?" Gary would plead. Even telling him we knew it was real to him, didn't satisfy him. "Ryan, you could learn to live with it and not let it take over your life. There are hearing aids and sign language." It was a daily struggle for everyone; for us, his family who tried so hard to help, but didn't know how. But mostly for Ryan, especially for Ryan, who struggled against horrible demons that none of us could see.

Peace was another world away for Ryan. He wrote in his journal, "There are rare moments in the day when I can say I am not consumed. Nothing I have tried has worked and I am running out of options." This hopelessness opened the door to what he perceived was the final option. His family never knew, nor did he give any clue that he was planning to end his life.

~Words from Ryan's Journals~

disillusionment, disappointment, done, finished, mediocre, ceased perfectionism, control, peace, excitement, unfulfilled life, lack of will to live further, detachment, apathy

These abstract words define who he had become by way of the total obsession with his hearing and inability to discern anything else. He said, "My brain could not be powerful enough to make me think I was going deaf if it weren't true." He could never understand why the hearing tests always came back normal. Even the ones that he did with his own audiology equipment at home showed only miniscule loss.

In spite of the obvious pain that Ryan was in, not even once did it occur to me that he would kill himself. Even though I had no answers to assuage his suffering, I believed he would be all right, somehow protected. An answer would surely come, though I had no idea how truly powerless I was to make a difference.

We deceive ourselves when we look only at the outside of things. If I had believed in mental illness, I might have known the subtle seductive force that had been slowing eroding Ryan's sense of himself. There was an insidious 'something' that was taking him away from the family and friends who loved him. If I had believed in mental illness I would have recognized the shrinking of Ryan's life as a signpost with a much darker source than mere growing pains. He said he had tried so hard to be 'normal' and only wanted the preoccupation with his ears to go away. This unknown and unnamed thing grew out of control, taking on a life of its own until it extinguished Ryan's. He decided it had robbed his life long enough.

Ryan's Journal

"Please trust me when I say that I did not want to die. There just was no other way out. I did not want to live the life of a hearing-impaired person. It's not fun, it's not interesting, and it's just a burden. Hearing loss is one of the great hidden menaces in life. Sometimes in people's lives there comes a time where the sadness just outweighs the happiness by a large amount. Some can overcome these times, Lord knows, I have overcome my share. But, I am finished. I have no more resources left to continue. I hope you all understand that I did not want to hurt you, but only to end my own pain."

Following the suicide of her husband, suicide survivor and author Carla Fine wrote in *No Time to Say Goodbye*, "Humans must relinquish the human conceit that we can change the people we care about and keep them alive through our love. We find ourselves beginning to understand the true, solitary nature of death."

What happened to Ryan after the suicide? I heard the worry in the voices of some well-meaning friends. The idea that suicide was somehow the unforgiveable sin seemed paramount.

I never once believed God had ever condemned Ryan. But, hearing the worry in my friends' voices, I became keenly aware of an all too familiar frantic confusion, rising up. My breath became shallow and I had to fight off the feeling of being strangled. What did God think about suicide?

In the Bible I read of seven suicides and one attempted suicide. But there is nothing about God condemning the person. So where had this idea arisen? I was driven to read more of the historical context surrounding suicide. The simplest definition of suicide is self-murder. It is sin like other sins. Historically, suicide became a dogma of the church through a heretical group called the Donatists who opposed the intermingling of church and state. Fanatical, they goaded church authorities into killing them, believing that this would secure a place in Heaven. To correct this heresy St. Augustine of Hippo wrote arguments making it a sin against the Church to commit suicide. St. Thomas Aquinas also condemned suicide based on the writings of Aristotle, Socrates, and Plato. Aristotle's *Nichomachean Ethic*, states that suicide is wrong because it is contrary to the natural life asserting purpose for humans.

Both Aquinas and Augustine claimed suicide violated God's law. Aquinas adds to Aristotle's ideas by stating that an obligation of love and charity for oneself precludes suicide, and that suicide is self-hatred. His argument is that society is harmed, and likens it to stealing from God since our lives are owned by God. Suicide did not become a crime under English Common Law until the Dark Ages.

Yes, our lives belong to God. This I believed. But, the issue was not the legality of suicide in God's eyes, but whether I still believed in His goodness. *How does a good God let bad things happen? I had presumed that somehow my family would be exempt from suffering of this magnitude.* And never before had I wrestled with or tried to reconcile suffering with my faith. I was overwhelmed and sad, and the journey seemed so hard, yet I yearned for some kind of peace and had to find something to satisfy my soul. Knowing God is in control after suicide seemed impossible: but how else would I ever make sense of this horrible thing?

My husband and I believe that Ryan's suicide was a direct result of the mental illness that afflicted him. The stigma attached to the words *mental illness* is such that no one would dare accept it if there were any other explanation for the pain. It was not a normal way of dealing with stress. Ryan truly wanted to end his pain, not inflict us with more. Carla Fine says, "Survivors will always cry for the missed chance, for the hindsight that proves so illuminating now that it's too late. We will always be filled with regret and always wish for a happy ending."

It was not a happy ending for Ryan on earth, but that's not the end of Ryan's story. What I ultimately believe about Ryan and about God is what will determine what my life will become. Can I accept that I could not have stopped Ryan from doing what he believed he must do? That it was the irrationality of the illness that became his logic? And that I could not have altered my actions or myself? I believe I must accept the forgiveness of God for my perceived failures and accept what cannot be changed even as I make a conscious choice to find meaning, purpose, and even happiness again.

"Our Last Walk"

Last Sunday evening I asked you to take a walk with me.
"Of course," you said as you pulled on your gray shorts.
The dogs were waiting at the door, anxious for their evening exercise.
They ran ahead sniffing as dogs do—
We didn't say much—I had learned to accept that we didn't talk
much anymore—Well, I talked and you listened.
You were unable to talk of anything else but the impending
deterioration of your ears.
"Ten minutes a day is all you can talk about it," I said.
You agreed. You didn't want to burden us anymore, you said.
But the walk . . . ah, the walk.
Was it a moonlit night, were the stars shining and signaling
ever brighter calling you Home?
God already knew your heart; I knew nothing.
But, you saved that last walk for me.
I look forward with longing to another walk we will take on
a different, more glorious day.
Perhaps we will walk around the river of life or the sea of glass.
Will you save the first walk for me?
Desiree Woodland © 2006

Chapter Two

JOURNEY'S END

Lay down your sweet and weary head, night has fallen;
you have come to journey's end.

People who suffer with mental illness are due dignity as every other human being. Mental illness does not change the essence of a person; in fact it often accompanies giftedness. Giftedness is the combining of previous ideas into new and useful combinations. Some people considered gifted who had mental illnesses are Vincent Van Gogh, Edgar Allan Poe, Emily Dickinson, Ernest Hemingway and Charles Schultz. These artists created beauty in the world while battling terrible depressions and anxieties—effects of mental illness.

The pain of giftedness or creativity or consciousness create a deep groaning in the human spirit, a deep crying out of the soul, as one goes deeper which involves a leaving behind. Scott M. Peck

All mothers think their children are the most gifted and talented, and I am no exception. Ryan was always a deep and thoughtful thinker. He wrote of himself:

"I was always a different child, highly sensitive and highly intelligent. Early on my mother taught me to read at age four. Books were a good escape. I always had friends, and I think children were intrigued by my quiet personality. I used to be a good artist, but gave that all up when I found the medium of mediums . . . music. Music played through a superior stereo could blast through depressions, wake up unknown talents and take you on journeys around the world."

Like most young boys, Ryan was utterly fascinated with machines. I remember as a fourth grader he challenged himself to create a unique entry for the Science Fair Invention Convention. His idea was very practical since he was tired of throwing balls over and over again to his dog Smokey. With a little metal, wood, wire and a net he created a machine that only required the flick of a lever and balls would shoot out into the yard. The hard part was teaching Smokey to bring them back!

As he grew, so did his interests, to include engineering, car design, stereo and speaker design, and anything musical. In middle school he played the trumpet and joined the Jazz Band.

These were years filled with the joy of living and new discoveries, including girls. Ryan had many friends, both boys and girls, because he was the quiet type with a respectful, thoughtful manner. He dreamed of being a DJ, scratching tunes, recording beats and playing with a band. He did have a band for several years, with rehearsals held wherever the parents allowed. Through the years the group practiced in our shed, and in friend's basements or living rooms. The members changed periodically, but Ryan was always in the middle of it. They played for their middle school dance and were in the Battle of the Bands in high school. These were some of Ryan's best days.

Ryan's Journal

"I became drawn at an early age to electronic audio equipment and to music. The sounds were spectacular, and I had the best sound system I could afford from the age of eight onward. Also, musical instruments, specifically the trumpet and bass guitar were huge parts of my development. I was later turned on to electronic music (turntables, samplers, keyboards). As soon as I found music I found audio equipment that was bigger and louder was better. You may remember my obsession with any and all kinds of sound equipment and bass. All of these things, playing music, designing speaker systems, writing music with my friends, listening to music by myself or with others, buying and looking at any kind of electronics are some of my favorite things. Most of my friends were the same way. Sure, I had other interests/friends, but this was to be my life's work."

During high school, he developed another love. Cars! He read anything and everything about them. Repair manuals and stereo magazines filled with complex and confusing terms were a joy for him to read. He took pride in being able to understand the technical aspects of mechanics. Our back yard was filled with remnants of his car education.

It was during late high school when those things I had easily explained away before began to look like symptoms, but of what I did not know. Things like hanging out with friends and skateboarding were becoming increasingly difficult for him to enjoy. The loud noise of the wheels against the concrete bothered his sensitive ears. His preoccupation with his sense of hearing was a worry to me as he became increasingly less involved with the friends who skated since he could barely tolerate the noise from wheels on cement. So I worried some more. But again, I normalized this strange obsession and hoped for the best because there was nothing that doctors could find to indicate any hearing loss. He still put stereos in all of his friends' vehicles, pushing through the anxiety over the perceived hazard for his ears. Ryan was the stereo expert: anything related to sound systems, music, D.J., all Ryan's expertise, and he was known to all of his friends as such.

In spite of his obsession, he continued to prove his technical expertise and learned to take out car engines, repair or replace them, diagnose car problems and do body work. It was a blessing to have my own private mechanic—one that I trusted implicitly with the upkeep on my car.

Once, Ryan had dreamt of making a real difference in the world. Always admiring those with unique ideas, he strove to be a person of originality. Ryan loved forming his own opinions on everything from war, religion, politics and alternative forms of government, especially philosophy and the meaning of life. He always tried to be a well-rounded person and developed thought-provoking ideas and opinions on many issues. Explaining these abstract ideas and trying to convince someone to change their point of view was a challenge he loved.

"Ordinary people find no difference between men."

We could sit for hours at Starbucks and talk about the existence of God. The reasons could be scientific, spiritual, mechanistic, or just plain practical, but he wanted to understand. He strove to listen to the voice of reason, which he said, would make one believe. "Everything on earth bears the stamp of a hidden God." He collected quotes that had meaning for him and added these to knowledge of issues he loved. Ryan had never been content with the answer, *because I said so*. He wanted to know why something should be done a certain way. Never disrespectful in his questioning or his response, he would accept the answer even if he didn't agree, as long as he understood why.

"Mom, you're a teacher. What do you think about the educational system in the US? It is teachers who know how to organize and sift through information to find the most important knowledge to teach. They are the ones who should be running the country instead of the government!"

He was a deep and thoughtful thinker all the days of his life except near the end. The wide range of topics he had once liked to debate was shrinking, for Ryan was on the edge of an illness that would soon take over. Instead of philosophy, human relationships or relationship with God, his arguments became about tax evasion, or how the IRS was illegal, or the American right to a citizen's militia and other un-Ryan-like ideas. I did not take him seriously, but wondered where these bizarre thoughts were coming from. Months before the psychotic break he was unable to engage in abstract thinking or any of the other thousand things that had made him Ryan.

Even though he refused to believe he had a mental illness, he submitted to the regimen of medications after checking out their side effects. I believe he submitted because the terror of actually having been admitted to a psychiatric hospital was so unbelievable. He applied for and received social security disability payments, and was once again able to pay his bills. I thought no longer having to worry about finances would help. At first it was a great relief, but mental illness was now stealing away his feeling of productivity. He had been unable to work because of the obsession and now there was more time to dwell upon it. He was heavily weighed down and trapped in such a small life. He never let on how much it affected him, but his journals tell the story. This quote by Vincent Van Gogh was in his notebooks, and I am distressed to think of him reading it and seeing himself in Vincent's words:

There is a great difference between one idler and another idler. There is someone who is an idler out of laziness and lack of character, owing to the baseness of his nature. If you like, you may take me for one of those. Then there is the other kind of idler, the idler despite himself, who is inwardly consumed by a great longing for some action who does nothing because his hands are tied, because he is so to speak, imprisoned somewhere, because he lacks what he needs to be productive, because disastrous circumstances have brought him forcibly to this end. Such a one does not always know what he can do, but he nevertheless instinctively feels I am good for something! My existence is not without reason! I know I could be quite a different person! How can I be of use, how can I be of service? There is something inside me, but what can it be? He is quite another idler. If you like you may take me for one of those.

Tragically, the feeling that he was no longer a functioning member of society, added to his depression. His journals indicate further how useless he felt since he was unable to work, could no longer help others, and wasn't even able to live independently because of his preoccupation with hearing loss.

I forced myself to read his self-deprecating, self-loathing and fearful words: "Self doubt paralyzes me and seems all consuming. The highs of life only last as long as I can turn off my brain. I'm so tired of living this way. I hate being afraid of everything, of not thinking I'm capable and doubting my every move. I just want some calm in my head. Some belief in myself." I wept to read his words. I never knew the darkness of his mental state. There were pages and pages of statements like these: "I will overcome." "I will develop social skills." "I will start believing in myself." "I will have a complete recovery of balance and hearing function."

Ryan was very hard on himself in his last months. It is true when people write in journals their feelings are often distorted and many people write that way when they are feeling down. I screamed out, though he would never hear: *You say you can't do things right and you are too sensitive and have an overactive imagination. As you were in that level of despair did you ever think about talking about it? Why couldn't you have told me? The feelings of your inadequacy were never shared. Perhaps you were ashamed. You were struggling with the horrible pain of your own worth and value which you could no longer grasp. When depression strikes one's soul, it strikes with a vengeance.* After the diagnosis in August 2005 until his death in May 2006 he was researching how to commit suicide. How could I have not known?

When the doctors asked him if he felt suicidal he brushed off the question as if it were the furthest thing from his mind. Ryan looked me in the eye and said, "I would never kill myself." I believed his words.

I could not even begin to grasp that the delusion of going deaf would become stronger and more powerful than life itself. Our brains are powerful, complex, wonderful creations; but if broken, can create a prison out of a once productive, full-of-promise life. I believe Ryan knew how ill his brain was, and he could no longer tolerate living without the health and vitality

he once knew. This quote from his journal speaks to me of the differentness
that he perceived in himself:

> *The truly creative mind in any field is no more than this:*
> *A human creature born abnormally, inhumanely sensitive.*
> *To them . . . a touch is a blow; a sound is a noise, a misfortune*
> *is a tragedy, a joy is an ecstasy, a friend is a lover, a lover*
> *is a god, and failure is death. Add to this cruelly delicate organism*
> *the overpowering necessity to create, create, create—so that without*
> *the creating of music or poetry or books or buildings or something of*
> *meaning, their very breath is cut off . . .*
> *They must create, must pour out creation.*
> *By some strange, unknown, inward urgency they are not really alive*
> *unless they are creating.*
> Pearl Buck

The question of 'why' haunts many survivors. With a note, one final
connection, we think it might answer the unanswerable. But, no answer
will ever be complete enough.

What Ryan's journals did give us was a window into his thinking and
distorted reasoning. He hoped we would understand his reasons for not
wanting to go on living, and to reassure us of his love and absolve us of any
guilt. I think Ryan was weary of trying to pretend he was still the person
he had once been. Now, his family was left in a 'new reality' to learn to be
people we had never been before.

Ryan's Journal

"I chose to end my life because of an unbearable affliction for which
there is no cure. It was not a rash or hasty decision. I survived for
as long as I did these past couple of months because of you guys.
You carried me. Thank you for all you did for me in these months,
and always. I only wanted to live normally again."

The symptom of Ryan's illness that is saddest for me and the most
devastating to him was the loss of music. A quote he loved said," Truth
can penetrate your heart, in a way that mere words cannot." I believe, as
he did, that music is the gateway to the spirit. Fragments from many songs
have ministered to me in my grief . . . "As my heart holds you, just one beat

away." "I believe that love will live on and never leave." Bittersweet words for the bittersweet longing of losing him. He had found the *medium of all mediums—music—truly a God-appointed gift*. We shall allow this gift of music, which Ryan believed could no longer minister to him, to minister to us in his stead and to heal our hearts, as it was unable to heal his.

I often needed music to minister to me. Many days I brewed a cup of tea and spent time in Ryan's room. Each time I walked across the breezeway separating his room from the rest of the house, I remembered that day. But I needed to be in his room, with his things, in the last place he was alive, in order to drown myself in music with melodies and lyrics that seemed to pierce the veil between heaven and earth.

I closed my eyes and listened to one song after another: Pachebel's *Canon in D*; *Navigatio,* a Celtic hymn about being at the edge of the earth and finding a door; *Homesick,* a song by Mercy Me; songs by Counting Crows and Weezer; Bob Marley and the sweet song from Forest Gump, the one that Ryan used to play on the piano. These songs allowed the sadness to drain out, even if only for a few moments.

Annie Lennox's words from *Into the West* also soothed me in the first long days and nights after Ryan died, and they still do—*Lay down your sweet and weary head. You have come to journey's end.* Be at peace dear Ryan.

"Threshold"

Your mind unable to see past the delusion, your body tired of the daily struggle, lay on the threshold.

On the threshold of your room I see your tent folded up, spirit gone.

I cannot fathom the meaning of this awful thing.

Give me time to process, give me time to grieve,
give me the Gift of time to comprehend this thing.

I see the threshold of a new life promised by God,
free of struggle and suffering.

Our lives on earth are only the threshold of our lives to come.

Desiree Woodland © 2006

Chapter Three

TELLING THE STORIES

On life's journey God gives the gift of endurance when we think we can't go on. This kind of learning is hard work, and a work in progress. He gives the power to do this work because His love will not leave us in our ignorance. Learning to accept that one's child has a serious illness or accepting that they died by suicide is the work of a lifetime.

Even when death comes in Nature's order of parent and *then* child, we realize instinctively that the ties that bind us to one other and to earth are intricate and fragile. But we still often live as if those delicate strands will never be severed. Death surprises us with its intensity.

Several months before Ryan was diagnosed with mental illness, my mother was diagnosed with Alzheimer's. Ryan spent countless hours researching what changes the illness would leave in its wake and how to best help her. The irony was that his life would soon be over, and hers, slowly stripped away. She could not comfort me with her wisdom and eternal perspective; the illness had robbed her too deeply. Self-pity raised its ugly head and sometimes I let it win.

I felt so small and alone in the darkness of this new life without Ryan, and I longed to share my burdens with my mother. They were unwieldy and heavy to carry without her. I didn't think she could comprehend what had happened to Ryan, but surprisingly one day while caring for her, I was given a gift of grace bigger than my own self pity. Mom had not spoken for weeks, and then out of nowhere a look came over her face and she asked a coherent question about 'my son' and then remarked: "He's always with you, isn't he?" *Oh yes, Mom he's always with me.*

Death is part of life they say. Then why does it feel like such an intruder? Following on the heels of Ryan's death, another intruder was lurking in the wings. Gary's mother never awoke from surgery because the doctors found cancer throughout her body. "We're sorry. We'll just have to hope for the best." On Mother's Day that year, only a week after we buried Ryan, we gathered at her bedside to pray, and gave permission to unhook the machines that were barely keeping her body functioning. Her spirit had long gone. We comforted ourselves with this thought: Now Grandma has the relationship with Ryan she'd always wanted.

But how much death can hearts hold? Sorrow multiplied upon sorrow. Every death deserves its own grieving and now grief had become tangled up. Our minds were numb and we were not sure we could ever sort it out.

Life is a story and each story will eventually include loss. Framing our losses into a narrative became a way to continue the bonds we had with our loved ones while they were alive. Ryan's grandmothers' stories are deeply woven into his. But loss is only part of the story. Someday, I believed, there would be a restorative story as well.

I hated myself for what I didn't know and couldn't protect Ryan from. I needed relief from the litany of accusations that seared my brain. I needed self-compassion and patience in order to learn how to process and adapt, before I could ever hope to create a restorative story. As parents we think part of our responsibility is to know everything, fix every problem and keep our children safe. But it is only an illusion, because we do not have that power. We can only do what is in our human ability, but after that we must trust them to a power greater than ourselves—God—there are just too many things we cannot save them from.

"You're Not Here with Me Now"

Child, you're not here with me now.
And the separation feels lonelier,
the ache is deeper,
and the yawning gap between us seems so wide.
For you, my child went Home before me.
Is there nothing that can soothe this immeasurable pain?
I look at your photo and imagine what you would look like now
If you had been a healthy, wholly complete man.

Child, you're not here with me now.
What did God have in mind when He created you?
He must have known the calamity that awaited you in the prime
of your life.
How His heart must have ached, as mine does now,
for the pain He knew you would suffer.
I believe His love went deeper,
His blood flowed freely, and His grace penetrated the walls of time
to grasp your hand as you left this world.
For the peace that you longed for was another world away.

Child, you're not here with me now.
And my heart is not whole.
I wait through the measure of my days
Learning to live again.
I will live again 'til time, for me, is no more.
And I'll reach through that veil of separation
To eagerly grasp your hand as you lead me to the Throne of God's Grace
And together we will understand the inscrutable mystery of our
lives and where, my child, we shall never be separated again.

Desiree Woodland ©2006

After he died many of Ryan's old friends from middle and high school, even elementary school came to visit. Following the death of a child, parents are hungry for a tangible way to hold onto those connections. We ask, *what did my child mean to you?* It is a gift to know they were loved by others and their life counted.

His friends were eager to share their memories of him. I think they knew their words were strands that connected us, and I was drawn into a deeper sense of knowing that no matter the length of life and whether or not we achieve success, we touch each other on the journey and can leave a lasting impression. Haley, a middle and high school friend said, "I will always remember that Ryan brought countless hours of fun to our house. I will think about what good times we all had playing together as kids."

John, a friend from elementary school said, "A memory I have of Ryan is that he was so innovative and creative. He seemed to walk slightly above all of us creatively, in a way forging the path and showing us the way to some new creative beat or hip hop group. He had a style all his own with magnetism about him. I always enjoyed spending time with Ryan, be it skateboarding, listening to music or just chatting with him. His creativity and uniqueness will be greatly missed."

Chris, a life-long friend said, "Ryan is the best of friends that I have ever had and will ever have. I have a special place in my heart just for him and only him because I need room for all of the great memories we shared and I never want them to be clouded or lost. There are few people in my life that have meant what Ryan meant to me, he was not only a friend, but a brother I never had and I will never forget him."

Another school friend said, "One of the most mechanically inclined and well-grounded friends I've had is Ryan. His genuine respect for people he cared about was easily recognizable. We shared similar interests in many things, from cars to stereo systems. His knowledge in these areas was far beyond the typical person who had twice his experience. He was a great guy and I will miss him dearly. I am fortunate to have been his friend."

Ricky, a friend from middle and high school said, "He is in a place far away from his daily struggle where he is without pain."

At first when I told Ryan's story it was traumatic and surreal. My son had been ripped from this life and I was angry. I was sad and confused, and so was my story. And I continued to recount the entire trauma, until I was spent and exhausted. I longed for another way to remember him. I was ready to begin to create the restorative retelling in which I could look at Ryan's whole life and try to see myself, Gary, and Michelle, not in the context of only the bad memories, but the good as well. Perhaps, instead of making a complete recovery, what we could hope for was an acceptance of how we had changed.

I am only just beginning to see myself in the narrative and context of Ryan's *entire* life. This process will never really be complete. The enormous sadness of his illness and death are overwhelming, but despite the struggle, I continue to work to gain some understanding and perspective. This book is my perspective.

Chapter Four

JOURNEY INTO MENTAL ILLNESS

For many families the process of finding medications and a treatment plan that works can be long and arduous. There is a maze of medications, treatments and information to digest. Shortly after Ryan's diagnosis, Gary and I attended the National Alliance for the Mentally Ill class, with the goal of learning how to navigate this maze. Called Family to Family, it is a sixteen week course on mental illnesses such as schizophrenia, bipolar disorder, and delusional disorder. It was unfamiliar territory and we were confused because Ryan didn't seem to fit any of the categories. Something was wrong, yes, but we were in denial. We did not want to believe that our son was severely disabled and or that he would not 'get over it' in time.

Sitting across from us the night of that first class was a couple who looked to be our age and whose story sounded eerily familiar. Describing their son's behavior they told of an obsession with physical symptoms that were not based in reality. *What's his diagnosis? Schizophrenia with affective disorder?* It was a sad and strange relief to hear their story; we were not alone. *Is your son getting better? What medications is he on? Who's his psychiatrist?*

Gary and I were in a fog, but no longer alone. Neither family was certain *if* or *what* might break through these powerful delusions. While we continued to attend classes Ryan began receiving a cocktail of medications we had never heard of while seeing the psychiatrist regularly. We thought it would be enough.

But it was not enough.

After Ryan died, I became driven to educate myself more about mental illness. I had not wanted to align myself with the sad sorrow that many people live each day. Education helped to relieve some of the guilt over my lack of understanding of the ramifications that a mental illness diagnosis brings. I talked with experts, watched movies, and read anything that might help me learn what I hadn't learned before. Mental illness is a biochemical illness, but because of its nature not easily identified. As a society we don't know how to deal with people who see things that aren't there, hear things that aren't there, or like Ryan feel things in their own bodies that aren't there. His mind and body became a prison. Not to be at home in the world, and not to even be at home in one's own body is a torment that only those who experience such a disruption in brain chemistry can understand.

I craved a conversation with people who did understand. Two autobiographies about schizophrenia that made a significant difference for me were *The Quiet Room* and *Divided Minds*.

The Quiet Room by Lori Schiller and Amanda Bennet tells of Lori's descent into mental illness with constant hallucinations and hearing voices. Through trial and error her doctors search to find a medication that works. Lori is subjected to many drug trials and hospitalizations until nine years later the drug Clozapine comes on the market. She responds favorably to it, but her psychiatrist warns that it is not a cure. She will probably still have the hallucinations and delusions, but now she can begin to cope with them. The future she once dreamed of is now traded for a life that is at least better than what she had been living.

Twin sisters, Pamela and Carolyn Wagner, together wrote *Divided Minds*. Both bright college women with promising futures, until Pamela (Pammy) becomes afflicted. I am saddened by this story of a once vigorous contributing member of society who graduates with honors from Brown University, but is unable to live out the dreams that she once held. Carolyn becomes a psychiatrist and this helps her learn how to live with her sister's illness. The reality of schizophrenia as a family illness is revealed through Carolyn and Pammy's combined insight.

Lori and Pammy had similar experiences, but each had individual symptoms. Ryan's symptoms were similar to theirs, but uniquely individual. The common thread is the very real difficulty of living with the knowledge that one's brain has changed.

In *Understanding Schizophrenia* psychiatrists Richard Keefe and Phillip Harvey offer a theory as to why the delusions and/ or hallucinations differ from person to person. They state:

> "All normal and disturbed people have inner lives involving
> their own wishes, needs, conflicts, and concerns. This inner

life influences everyone but in a minor way. In psychosis this inner life gets elaborated, twisted up and down and dominates their understanding of the outer world."

This sheds new light on the delusion that took Ryan's life. Since he loved music so much, and wrote that it had the power to lift his spirits, I believe that is why it took the form of deafness. But the delusion didn't just show up one day, it was a slow, painful progression. But on the day it took his life, it moved with such force and ferocity that any shred of logic cowered in its presence.

Ryan's Journal

"I couldn't live without my hearing. I couldn't be happy without my good hearing. If I'm not happy and I can't function, I'm just a burden. I'm sorry Mom and Dad and Michelle. I'm so weak. I couldn't handle it anymore. I'm so sorry."

After high school he worked for one year before he admitted that becoming an engineer would not be possible. It was too much for him to deal with, and we didn't yet understand why. With parental prodding, he left for Phoenix to attend mechanics school instead. He worked part time, attended school full time and drove home to Albuquerque on the weekends. It would have been an exhausting schedule for anyone. After the first semester he asked to move back home because his ears had become ultra sensitive to noise, he said. The mechanics tools were too loud, and he felt he knew more than the teachers, so he moved back home without a plan for his future. We weren't happy with his lack of a plan, but he was 20 years old by this time and old enough to decide the path his future would take. Our job was to stand by and support him.

Each time there was a change of plans, our hopes for his future died a little too. Instead of being an engineer or a licensed mechanic, he would become an entrepreneur. He still enjoyed working on cars. To save up money for his business, he worked at a local grocery store where a long time friend was his boss. In spite of being grateful for a job and grateful for the friendship, he felt his ears were being compromised. However, the job did allow him to develop a few other friendships, and occasionally they would all work on cars together. He was forced to be part of society. There was little else that he loved more than buying a car for cheap, repairing it and selling it at a profit! This he could do in spite of his apprehensions. He knew all the related businesses to help him in his used car business. He scoured newspapers for car deals and would haul, drag or push them home. Our backyard looked like a used car graveyard.

After working at the store for as long as he felt his ears could stand, he gave his notice. After all, he was making some money with the car business now and seemed satisfied to work alone. There would be no loud music and he could control the noise level.

Since the preoccupation kept increasing, eventually his friends stopped coming by or calling. And as he became more isolated, he did not return their phone calls or see them for more than a few minutes at a time. It was excruciating to stand by, without a clue as to what was wrong, and watch him slowly being snatched away.

All parents want their children to be independent, so to help him regain a sense of his life we pushed him to move into his own place; after all by now he was going on 24 years of age. I clearly remember sitting with him as he cried with such intense emotion as I had never seen. Putting his head on my lap he begged, "Please don't make me go. Please." *But we were supporting him by making him do what he did not want to do, weren't we? He needed to grow up didn't he?* The apartment was only blocks away and we could see each other often. I could not relate nor understand the level of his pain and my heart bleeds to think that I couldn't recognize it as a mental disorder. Trying to make it seem like a grand adventure, we painted, cleaned and shopped for his new place. But it was only the place where he slept. He spent his days, while his dad and I were at work, at our home working on the computer and goofing around with car stuff, until the psychotic break brought him back home for good. With brutal intensity it showed what mental illness could do to a person.

I draw back in horror at the idea that the reason for Ryan's arrested development was mental illness. No, actually, I am grateful there is a name for such sadness. I see it now. The blinders I had on before were only because of my naiveté of the illness.

The journey of mental illness really started for Ryan at age 19. No one knew there was a disease lying dormant in his brain that would forever change the course of his life, and ours. But, in hindsight I see how he was changing. His dreams, his aspirations and outlook for the future were shrinking. We, his family, had accepted his quieter, more sensitive personality; all those qualities had made him such an endearing child, but now had become more pronounced. He began to be obsessive about a ringing in his ears and complained of hearing loss.

Through the next few years the illness progressed until the perceived hearing loss was the only thing in his life. Ryan seemed unable to exhibit any control over his thoughts. What was this strange behavior? There was never any acting out, anger, or other more obvious signs that may have sent up a warning flag. His pain was all internalized.

Mental illnesses cannot yet be seen with a blood test or a scan, but must be diagnosed by behavior and thinking alone. So when Ryan was diagnosed with possible schizophrenia and/or delusional disorder, I was relieved there was a name for his arrested development. I cried, I moaned, I thanked God that now he could be helped. And so I left it to the professionals, the experts at the hospital. The diagnosis made me numb and so I trusted them, in spite of the vague sense of impending uncertainty on this unknown path.

The road to full-blown schizophrenia is always paved with other symptoms like social anxiety, self-doubt, or thoughts of not fitting in. Alone they do not indicate severe mental illness, but these precursors are always present if the illness takes its prescribed path. *Yes, these were issues that Ryan had struggled with, but don't we all?*

I think about some of the things that were hard for Ryan as he was growing up; he was always a bit shy, had a sensitive nature, he dreaded each new school year, and cried deeply over the loss of pets. This describes a beautiful sensitive person, not abnormal. But, I think these things cut deeper and hurt longer than I knew.

I believe the thought of going out into the world and facing it was more than he could handle because he was locked in a mind with a life of its own. Oh, how I wish I could have shared this burden with him. He was so alone, but yet he was not alone.

God, you were with him in this despair. Outwardly, I saw Ryan struggle to deal with his life. He called on You but said he could no longer feel Your presence, especially that last year. But Ryan belonged to You. Your presence was evident in the laughter, the tears, the struggles and the love of family life. And I believe angels surrounded him and that somehow he knew divine comfort deep within his spirit, a place deeper than the illness, a place I could not reach.

The psychiatrists did the best they could. Families are desperate for help when mental illness is part of the diagnosis, and there is increased pressure for a quick fix. Pressure comes from the suffering person, the family who wants to believe that a pill could bring their loved one back, and the psychiatrists who see such unimaginable suffering. The team of doctors wanted Ryan to participate in clinical trials to better understand what was going on in his brain. There were any number of newer medications that could have been tried, but Ryan wouldn't cooperate. He refused to be a "guinea pig," and spent countless hours researching side effects. He was fearful, and adamant about protecting his ears, thus limiting their options.

In the mental health care system, after the age of 18, parents no longer have authority to make decisions for their child. I pleaded with and begged Ryan to participate, but the illness that made him so afraid would not allow his brain to respond to logic. *Was the diagnosis correct? Was he on the right medication, I wondered?*

Ryan was frantic with anxiety and had very little peace the entire nine months of treatment. At first, the medications seemed to calm him. But as time passed, it was evident they would not penetrate the delusion. I took notes on Ryan's behavior to share at doctor appointments: *January 2006: He hasn't eaten in several days, convinced that red meat is a factor preventing the Neomycin from coming out of his ears. He spends any available money on herb concoctions which he believes will stimulate hair cell regeneration. He won't sleep in his newly carpeted room because he believes the carpet fumes are detrimental to his hearing. He paces nervously and cannot seem to be still.*

I was completely out of answers, out of patience and almost out of faith. I couldn't get past his obsession in order to communicate with the sweet darling boy I'd given birth to and carried for nine months. The pain of labor from his birth seemed small in comparison with the labor of helping him get through this. Oh, how I hoped there would be an answer soon.

In early fall, before his diagnosis and hospitalization, we had driven to Flagstaff to see a faith healer, someone he found on the Internet. During the six-hour drive we discussed faith and how healing comes in God's time and in His way. He was determined that his ears would be restored, when I knew it wasn't his ears that needed healing. There was no change, and Ryan was greatly disappointed. I knew he needed God's touch, but not knowing for what. I continued to offer prayers daily.

After the diagnosis, Ryan continued to search for solutions to his hearing dilemma, still using the laser several times a day. In his desperation he even consulted a psychic healer. All of this while receiving psychiatric treatment. As I look back on the peculiarities of his final months, I see symptoms of acute mental illness: the lack of care for personal appearance, the overwhelming preoccupation with his ears, lack of logic with very little affect, refusal to eat more than chicken and cheese for fear the iron in the food would hurt his ears.

He believed in this loss with a strange passion, and there was always the sadness, as if he knew he was really and truly slipping away. His family was unable to engage with that sadness because shock and disbelief had consumed us.

Time can be a treacherous enemy and work against families blindsided by a diagnosis of mental illness and unfamiliarity with the mental health system. I was lost in a fog of agencies known only by acronyms and medications with unpronounceable names. Families need professionals who will offer assurance that there is someone invested in helping them and their loved one understand the implications of all that has happened.

Access to comprehensive mental health treatment is not easily obtained; indeed for those without insurance it can be even more difficult to acquire or to navigate the maze of medications, treatments, and mental health and government systems. There had been no choice about which hospital to take Ryan, because he had no insurance.

We became like robots. Unused to sickness or regular doctor appointments, we parked in the same parking space, we pushed the buzzer to open the same locked door and sat in the same waiting room, in the same seats as the time before. A nurse would call Ryan's name and we'd step into the doctor's office. We'd wait some more. And we'd hope. Hope that soon the medications would make a difference. Hope that this nightmare would end. This could not really be our lives. We struggled to hold on to that hope.

Ryan seemed to be in another world as he answered the same questions week after week. "No, I am not suicidal." "Yes, I know I need to get out, change my focus." "Yes, I am complying with taking my meds, but not all of them." "I don't need to take an antidepressant because if my ears were all right, I wouldn't be depressed." He had lost all hope of ever having normal hearing again.

A good analogy for mental illness is a broken brain. What is it like to live with a broken brain? "A person walking through normal life, with a loving family and friends, with plans for the future, suddenly encounters something awful. Slowly, seductively you become captive of a brain that won't let you connect anymore to the outside world. What is there in any person's experience to prepare them to cope with a broken brain? Who can understand what a catastrophe this break is for the human soul?" says Dr. Nancy Andreasen, in the *Broken Brain*.

Mental illness takes our loved ones away from reality and therefore away from the people who love them. It looks 'normal' to a degree, but its obsessive components can take over and essentially control more and more of a person's thoughts, unless medications can remedy the effects.

Ryan's Journal

"I used to take such pleasure in helping others, my friends especially, particularly when the help was required in an area where I had talent. I loved helping people."

These are connections Ryan had once enjoyed and loved. But now the total preoccupation with his ears would not allow him to do so. He suffered the isolation and loneliness, as well as the 'knowing' that something was wrong. How can a parent or psychiatrist understand the torture such a person is going through? Dr. Andreasen continues, "People with mental illness, particularly schizophrenia are locked out of the outside world, and locked inside their head with nothing but these out-of-control thoughts. What is broken is also the brain's ability to process emotions." Emotions that had once allowed Ryan to connect with family and friends could no longer be expressed because the delusion had become his reality.

In *Divided Minds* we read the lament of Pammy's heart: "I am not equal to the task of the terrible fatigue of living in the real world." Her sister Carolyn describes her during a visit to the state hospital, " . . . she avoids the cafeteria where she can't control the assault of incoming stimuli," and after a severe psychotic break for Pammy in middle age Carolyn says, "I can't imagine living the way Pammy does. What right do I have to insist that she stay alive?"

These quotes connect me to Ryan because I relate to feelings about a brilliant creative person becoming severely ill and the illness changing the person they were meant to be.

Suicide connected to schizophrenia is misunderstood. First of all, people with schizophrenia have the highest suicide rate. Is it any wonder why? It is a physiological as well as a psychological disorder characterized by beliefs and delusions that are perceived by the brain as reality. There can be hallucinations and other disturbances in thinking and communicating, as well as the deterioration of a person's social functioning, leaving behind a lost sense of self. This is not living. *I say that my son left the earth too soon, but should not judged for the illness that he did not deserve, that no one deserves.* The pain of watching him lose himself was so great: as great as the sadness of him not being here.

Medication can tone down symptoms, but not cure them. In part this leads to the stigma surrounding mental illness. Particularly with schizophrenia there is additional misinformation regarding violence. According to the Surgeon General, the percentage of violence is no higher in persons with mental illness than the general population. But just the word *schizophrenia* can bring hysteria to the world at large.

There are as many ways of looking at this devastating illness as there are families whose loved ones are afflicted. Medications are improving: research goes on full force because of organizations like NARSAD (A leading charity dedicated to mental health research), and in my own state of New Mexico a world-class research facility called the UNM Mind Institute. Many people are helped with medication and therapy and I am grateful for every single avenue that supports people living with mental illness. Treatment programs like this allow individuals to move into the future, however warily, learning resiliency, self-care and to monitor the return of symptoms.

But what of those individuals who haven't yet found a medication to alleviate the most serious symptoms? And what if one is never found? What does life look like for them? Parents of children whose symptoms are severe and recurring live in constant sadness and ambiguity. They ask questions that begin with **if** or **why** or **when**, questions I no longer ask for my child, but for others' children. Parents often experience a struggle between the realities of daily life and faith for the future.

Answers don't come easily. *In fact, are there any real solutions to this illness that has so changed the people we thought our children could become? If we had understood, could we have halted the progression of the illness? Can we now learn to give up the struggle of trying to fix them?*

Somehow we must conclude that we are not in charge. We cannot alter the genetic course of our child's life.

"Cosmic Order"

A parent is invested in the life of their child
The sweetness of self—sacrificing love
But with great love comes great pain
There is an undoing of some cosmic order at work here
A child preceding a parent in death
It's not supposed to be this way

In whose hands are we?
Whose plan called for the death of my son so soon?
I am kicking and screaming, chafing under this burden
Yet, Death has come and I must face the cold hard fact.
Knowing that my Sovereign God loves Ryan
More than any earthly parent
Knowing that He sees the eternal picture
I cannot even comprehend
He asks me to trust Him in the dark
Because His ways are perfect and one day I will understand.

Desiree Woodland © 2006

Chapter Five

LIVING WITH WHAT IS

Circular thoughts repeat the endless litany of facts about mental illness. My personal experience forces me to do this, placing the facts in order, trying to regain a sense of peace about what happened to Ryan.

Mental illness takes many forms and disrupts life in many ways. Its presence is not easily detected as families try to figure out why there is something different about their loved one. It can raise its ugly head at any point during one's life time, but it is common for symptoms to manifest in adolescence or young adulthood. On a purely simplistic level it looks like an inability to deal with the stresses of life, but that places the responsibility upon the individual. No one *chooses* to get sick. To the outside observer it looks as if the runaway thoughts or unusual behaviors are within the control of the person. This is one of the difficulties in acknowledging that the illness even exists, much less being able to accept it. Mental illness is an illness of the brain as cancer is an illness of the cells, a physical sickness, a chemical imbalance. At its worst, it is a dark sad world that closes the sufferer off from friends and family; robbing them of their dignity, sense of self, and value to the rest of the world. And often, the signs of a young life going wrong can be almost imperceptible to parents who try to make excuses as well as make 'room in the world' for a child with changes in their personality. Parents think, "It's just a phase, he'll grow out of it. Surely he will come around and get his life together."

The National Alliance of the Mentally Ill defines mental illnesses as: "Disorders of the brain that can often profoundly disrupt a person's thinking, feeling, mood, and ability to relate to others. Mental illnesses include such disorders as bipolar disorder, schizophrenia, major depression, obsessive-compulsive disorder, anxiety disorders including Post-Traumatic Stress Disorder, and other severe and persistent mental illnesses."

Even for trained mental health professionals a unified agreement on a diagnosis can be difficult. Our brains are not fixed, but fluid. Thoughts flow in and out, and at times we can all have abnormal thinking. Analyzing one's own thinking takes place all the time. But when one suffers under the influence of a powerful delusion this does not happen.

Despite the best efforts of doctors, mental illness is still a mystery and how best to deal with it remains elusive. Very little is actually known *yet* about its causes or how to control it successfully with medication. Loved ones should be skeptical of any psychiatrist who advocates quick intervention strategies, or touts unusually high success rates. The diagnoses intertwine and overlap, as do the manifestations and intensities of the disease. What is usually agreed upon is that genetics play a large part, dictating when it manifests and how severely it progresses. Web research sites such as *www. schizophrenia.com* show possible connections with environmental factors such as a viral infection in utero or heavy marijuana usage. It is thought that schizophrenia may actually be several different illnesses combined.

Historically, treatment resistance has been a very serious issue for patients with schizophrenia. In *Understanding Schizophrenia* researchers Richard S.E. Keefe and Philip D. Harvey, say that more than 80 percent of people who have a single psychotic episode never recover, and many have increasingly severe symptoms with each successive episode. Medical care and knowledge are improving, but the elusive cure is still out of reach. Brain scans may yield some information, but even the best PET and MRI scans cannot help when significant treatments are not yet available. Drugs called neuroleptics (anti-psychotics) are prescribed for psychosis and treatment. These drugs are supposed to manage delusions and hallucinations as well as disordered thinking. The psychiatric model of mental illness has thankfully changed from a model of a *troubled mind* which cites inadequate parenting or a dysfunctional family, as the cause of mental illness, to the *broken brain* model that cites an abnormality in brain or chemistry structure.

I had not believed in mental illness, but now understanding its devastation, it is shameful that in the past, parents were blamed.

One is no longer 'normal' when diagnosed with a mental illness. The illness that changed Ryan never responded to treatment, despite a cocktail of anti-anxiety, anti-depression and anti-psychotic drugs. It wasn't until months after Ryan died that I learned it is common to try different drugs in order to find the right combination. But Ryan did not give us the gift of time to figure this out or even define the character of our obligations. *What must we as parents do? What must we not do?*

As the parent of an adult child in the mental health system, I was not privy to the necessary information that may have forced me to trust less in a magic cure and to fight for my son. Indeed, doctors shared very little information about mental illness with us. Living with Ryan during his toughest days, I no longer expected instant answers, but I wanted to know what they saw when they looked at him sitting in their office, wringing his hands, tears streaming down his face. Did *they* know he was lying about wanting to end his life? The doctors never held out hope for Ryan's recovery, or even improvement.

I am again overwhelmed by the burden of Ryan's suicide and my lack of understanding. I continue to torture myself with the notion that if some kind of drug or talking therapy had been provided to Ryan earlier in the progression of the disease, it might have been circumvented. I don't know if that is true or not, but I have suffered much by incorrectly assuming total responsibility for what I did not know. Unwarranted guilt floods over me. I am learning this guilt is undeserved, but it cuts to the heart. Bitter pills to swallow. All parents unintentionally scar their children in unseen ways that cannot always be undone.

Several years of our family's life were in *limbo*. Ryan's life was shrinking and we, like frogs in cold water, didn't realize the water was slowly beginning to boil until we were cooked. Trapped in a roiling cesspool we couldn't climb out nor did we know how to reduce the heat.

Occasional glimpses of the real Ryan surprised us with moments of pure delight. Like when the dogs' antics would elicit the soothing sound of his laughter, almost forgotten, and through my fears I dared to think he might get well after all. But the real Ryan couldn't shake the prison for long. It held him captive through the night when he couldn't sleep. It greeted him at dawn's first light.

What I had seen before as idiosyncrasy, but now as symptom, was not just the isolation from friends, but family as well. There were very few restaurants, family gatherings (unless forced) or other small outings where he would go, except Starbucks for green tea or to a park with the dogs. The music that soothed him was never listened to anymore. Each time a perceived lessening of hearing quality or ringing happened, he found something new to give up, until there was nothing left.

Ryan's Journal

"Thank you, Mom and Dad for everything you've ever done for me and all you went through with me these past few months. I knew this day was coming the moment I figured out what I had done to myself (the Neomycin). I have been thinking this over since the day I used the antibiotic. I know I have more to offer others and reasons not to kill myself, but I had to make a choice, and this was it."

How he functioned at all with long days filled with nothing but thoughts of his ears seems incomprehensible. The utter turmoil in his mind, and no way to let the people who loved him know what he was planning must have been a huge burden for him. Loved ones 'normalize' the unusual behavior they see in their ill family member. It was as though he had a terminal illness but we couldn't recognize it.

Quoting again from *Understanding Schizophrenia*, "Schizophrenia is a degradation of the brain's chemistry and the sufferer shows symptoms of isolation and distress, confusion and anxiety." Gungsadawn Kataikaru, a research student at Bryn Mawr, says that the sensory input systems of the brain are so altered in severe mental illness that there is an external time and internal time constancy that is lost. He says, "To lose constancy of time is to lose the basis of reality. Ten percent of those diagnosed with schizophrenia commit suicide. Not being able any longer to understand nor communicate with the outer world is lonely and so they turn to their own psychotic conscience." *www.serendip.brynmawr.edu* Yes, I can surely agree that Ryan lost not only the sense of time, but the entire basis for reality.

Each attempt to pull him out of the abyss and back to us usually became another dead end, even though I attended each psychiatric appointment with Ryan. In a letter I wrote to one of his doctors I expressed my gratitude for what they were doing to help my son . . . *I still have major concerns about him. Ryan is so preoccupied and dominated by the sense of loss that he has excluded everything else. He is quite unable to work and we are on a waiting list for Social Security benefits. In addition to his other medications, I think he should be on the antidepressant you prescribed. What else can I do to help him? I feel so helpless.*

In the *Burden of Sympathy*, Dr. Karp says, "There is no normative basis for understanding the behavior of the mentally ill family member." Reading this allows relief to flow over me. Knowing that I could not see what I didn't know, and that the confusion and numbness about what to feel before and after his diagnosis was a 'normal' response. Mental illness had separated us from our child and a brother from his sister. Its weapons of pain and isolation had wounded him, and our helplessness was magnified.

2006—after Ryan's death
Mother's Journal

Ryan, I am sad for the paucity of your life. It became so small and I didn't know how to help you enlarge it. No one did. It was the prison that no one could break into or out of. They say that animals can be an instrumental source of comfort in human pain. Our dogs Bailey and Scraps certainly gave you brief moments of respite, and I love them for that.

So, how does a parent live with a child who suffers from mental illness? The challenges faced by parents may differ from spouses or siblings, but the struggles of how to integrate these challenges may be quite similar. Dr. Karp says:

"Illness, because of its capacity to so thoroughly disrupt the coherence of daily life, demands ongoing assessments about proper boundaries between caregivers and consumers. When confronted with mental illness family members quickly learn that without constructing appropriate boundaries they risk becoming engulfed and potentially consumed by the other's illness. Sustaining an appropriate level of involvement is extraordinarily difficult. Partly this is true because of the intrinsic nature of mental illness. Not only is the course of the illness unpredictable, but also the ailing person may act unpredictably. It is hard enough for the healthy person to imagine the pain of a person who suffers from a physical illness they themselves have never experienced. It is quite another thing to understand a person who thinks and feels in ways that seem totally incomprehensible."

The Burden of Sympathy defines a credo called the 4 C's, written for people who suffer along with their family member. It says, *I didn't cause it, I can't cure it, I can't control it, all I can do is cope with it.* This is what we must cling to even in the face of great sadness. More bitter pills to swallow.

I remember reading in some pamphlet that I can no longer find, "Delusions are strange committed beliefs held only by the person diagnosed, who refuses to change the belief despite strong evidence to the contrary," This definition describes the struggle of trying to convince Ryan that he was not going deaf. Our helplessness was magnified each time we failed.

I have learned that mental illness varies in degree from mild to severe. It's divided into categories of mania, schizophrenia, dementia, and anxiety disorders, with many divisions within the categories. The DSM IV is the best diagnostic tool available and yet it is limited in offering a treatment plan and course of action. The illness manifests in many different ways making it difficult to diagnosis. What are the links? Are they genetic? Abnormalities during gestation? Environmental triggers? A virus? I think Ryan's illness will always be a mystery.

My message for family members and friends left behind or for those trying to help a loved one with chronic mental illness is *hold onto hope.* Hope can ease the burden when healing is not possible. We must endure, our loved ones must endure, but there is still hope. Hope that we will find threads of grace to help us bear and walk this road. It can be very isolating to live with someone who does not fit the norm, or whose behavior is out of control. The stigma and suffering of having unsettled thoughts and feelings, *through no fault of one's own,* is significant in a world that emphasizes achievement. Ryan had long since stopped achieving. Why didn't I see his lack of achievement as significant? In trying to answer questions like this I have become a student of my son. His journals have given insight into what I hadn't known before.

At times, I was nearly consumed with finding out what the experience of mental illness was like. One excruciatingly painful book called *An Unquiet Mind* is the story of psychologist Kay Jamison who suffers from bipolar disorder. She lets us into her private hell as she struggled to learn how to live with this horrible disease. Finding relief in lithium was life-changing, but as her symptoms came under control, she stopped taking it. This led to her one suicidal episode.

My heart aches with such knowledge.

Writing about the depths of her experience and pain she says:

"Depression: lack of confidence, self respect, the inability to enjoy life, to walk, talk or think normally, the exhaustion, the day terrors, the night terrors, to be slow of mind, no beliefs in the possibility of life, the pleasures of sex, the exquisiteness of music, or the ability to make yourself or others laugh. Clinical depression is flat, hollow, unendurable, tiresome, and tedious beyond belief."

The small changes in his late teens we attributed to growing pains:the slow disintegration of plans for a challenging future, the school failure during high school, the shrinking desire to be part of a social circle—all these things made us sad. After the diagnosis we understood no better as to why he was so obsessed with his hearing. We complained about his lack of attention to grooming, the strange diets, and we became accustomed to the hovering sense of hopelessness. Our family was no longer what it had been. We wanted Ryan back, mind and body, participating fully in life. There is no Pollyanna picture of mental illness; it is all a matter of individual body chemistry that determines the severity and deterioration of the illness. Its course is often unpredictable and frightening.

May 6, 2006 after Ryan's death
Mother's Journal

Deep sobs escape and flow out into air that Ryan no longer breathes. Ryan just wanted to be normal. We discovered that Ryan hadn't been taking his pills for at least 2 weeks, maybe more. (*When he was first diagnosed I had monitored his medication to be sure he was taking it.*) Oh the wave of guilt—almost as painful as when I found him. I knew no peace until I let Gary's words penetrate my heart, "Maybe he stopped taking them because he just wanted to be normal." Doctors told us that delusions are difficult to treat with medication, and Ryan was on the drug that had the highest success rate, but they didn't tell us that people with delusions have the highest suicide rate. I grind these words into my brain; Ryan just wanted to be normal, no pill, and no crutch.

It was love that caused Ryan to leave us words of comfort for the help we tried to give him during the worst days of his illness. "Please," he said, "Know that this was not your fault. You did everything in your power to help me and I appreciate all of it."
There is controversy among the mental health population about the importance of medications versus holistic remedies and other treatments such as acupuncture or diet alone. Medication is a life-saving necessity for most people which can dramatically stabilize brain chemistry. If the right medication can be found if makes a powerful difference in their quality

of life. Many afflicted people can, and do, still work with the help of medication and lead fulfilling, satisfying lives.

According to a recent National Alliance on Mental Illness (NAMI) newsletter, the average delay in entering treatment is nine years. I wonder if like Ryan, symptoms are perceived by the person as weakness, failure or something too 'abnormal' to reveal—even to a loving family. The family normalizes those attributes and accepts them as 'personality differences'. Of course, when people exhibit symptoms far beyond the limits of civility, symptoms that have social ramifications rather than internal, it is easier for families to recognize the seriousness of the problem and seek help.

Ryan felt he was living a sub-human existence and to him there was very little of his humanity left. Finding one's way in this world is challenging enough, but the complications of a severe mental illness made it impossible for Ryan.

Symptoms vary with each person, often overlapping, making it challenging to correctly diagnose the illness. Multiple symptoms can occur in different patterns, even in patients with the same diagnosis. I see this in Ryan's illness. It is my prayer that more knowledge and understanding of the brain will produce an antidote to the terrible blight that mental illness has created in once vibrant lives. Left untreated its implications exact a huge toll on society in the form of lost wages, criminalization, and early death. Additionally, chronic mental illness accounts for much of the homeless population.

This was the case for Stewart Govig, author of *Souls Are Made of Endurance*. This book tells of the difficult experiences he and his family endured with medication, housing issues, and the inevitable acceptance issues surrounding the diagnosis of his son Jay's mental illness. He says, "Suffering is neither punishment nor ennobling; it can however open possibilities for engaging with the theology of the cross." These words made me weep, but left me wondering about their truth. Would the cross ever be able to speak to me about Ryan's suffering? I read on and received courage from Govig's example. He speaks of endurance not as a race, but the way to finish the race. Quoting from a beautiful unpublished piece by Carl Sandburg, he says, "Take up your cross, and go the thorn way. And if a sponge of vinegar be passed you on a spear, take that too. Souls are made of endurance. God knows."

Living with a loved one who suffers from a chronic form of mental illness is like living in the Twilight Zone. The cost to families comes in the form of weariness, anxiety and sadness. From the *Broken Brain*, by Dr.

Nancy Andreasen, she says, "Watching one's child suffer the varied and painful symptoms of schizophrenia is an anguishing experience for parents, who often go from one doctor to another, hoping for a miracle cure. None exists yet. Psychiatrists who either discover a definitive treatment for, or identify major factors concerning it, will perhaps make the most important medical contribution of the twentieth century." This was written in 1985, and as yet there is still no cure. Gary and I thought that Ryan was at least on the way to recovery.

At one time anti-psychotics were seen as wonder drugs that might prevent progressive deterioration in some cases. But, often the percentages of those afflicted with schizophrenia who receive treatment are helped only 40% of the time. Those, like Ryan, who are not helped, become steadily more crippled by the obsession, and like Ryan, people who have obsessive/compulsive tendencies increase the likelihood that medication will not help.

9/24/06—after Ryan's death
Mother's Journal

Gary and I have just finished watching a film called *Schizophrenic*, produced by UCLA in 1990. It chronicles the life of Steve Peabody who suffers from schizophrenia. Steve agreed to be filmed longitudinally, and the film follows 10 years of his life from age 33 to 44. It begins by showing Steve on the streets of Los Angeles in the midst of a psychotic episode. But he has lived with this illness long enough to know to go for help. He enters the hospital and put on a stronger medication. While he is being interviewed we meet his family. They tried to normalize the strange behavior that Steve began to exhibit around 20 years of age. There is much sadness in his family because of how the illness has changed him. The medication does not cure his hallucinations even after the passage of time. He has a flat affect and survived one suicide attempt in which his thought process was that ending his life would be a good idea. He doubts that he will ever be *normal*, have a girlfriend, a job, or get married. He and his family have no doubt mourned the things he could have done had he not gotten this awful illness. Steve is tortured night and day with seeing things that are not there, voices in his head that don't stop, and the long days of not being productive because it is so overwhelming just to deal with the hallucinations. This film is one of the many stories of what mental illness can do, and it forces me to face how ill Ryan really was, and to know that I would not have wanted him to suffer this kind of existence.

Families suffer chronic sorrow when a child has a debilitating illness and parents mourn the loss of family structure. It can be difficult to define parental obligations to a child with mental illness, particularly when the child is an adult. What is clearly defined in other illnesses now seems muddied. Practical questions arise. Where will they live? Can they live independently? How much should parents be involved? What is the financial cost for taking care of a grown child? Will they always need help and support? How will they survive when I die? Questions like these haunted Gary and me because this was a chapter in our family's life that would never be written.

Sibling relationships can become strained, or almost nonexistent, as with Michelle and Ryan. Sometimes detached behavior threatens to sever a relationship, and for Ryan, working at relationships became too exhausting. It was not a question of love, but of survival. He left this note for his sister:

"We were very different growing up and I know we weren't close. But, I admire you as a person, I am so proud of your accomplishments, and I really love you. I was a very hard person to get to know, and I blame myself. You are the coolest sister anyone could have. I will see you again, and we'll talk then."

In my mind's eye I imagine the faces of two little children, wide smiles stretched across chubby cheeks, arms wrapped around each other. I sigh as I remember the good days of childhood when Michelle and Ryan were close.

Many families remain isolated even within the family circle. Feelings of shame are suffered in silence. Groups like NAMI offer support through classes that provide education, understanding and a sympathetic shoulder to lean upon. We grieved for dreams once held, now changed, just as surely as Ryan's life had changed.

Letting go is difficult for all parents. But I did not let go of a healthy son, who came to the edge of adulthood, whose heart was bursting to spread his wings and soar, but rather a son who came to the edge of adulthood desiring to fly and was prevented from soaring because of a brain disorder called mental illness.

Mental illness forces changes to our future. Parents cannot live their child's lives for them. It takes faith to let go, and it takes hope that God will take care of what we have given back to Him. How else can parents survive? Scott Peck wrote "Do not feel totally, personally, irrevocably responsible for everything. That's my job. Signed God." A parent of a son with a mental illness once said, "I had to come to a place of *powerlessness* and relinquish my ill child to God." Yes, we must all come to this place of endurance if we are to survive.

Lacking any sense of bravery, I speak Stuart Govig's words, "Trust your own heart; trust in the strength of God, for your soul too is made of endurance."

Though the journey may include pain, if we give ourselves permission to acknowledge the bad along with the good, endurance grows. Without shame, we seek the necessary professional, spiritual and community supports that allow us to deal with the reality of what has happened to our loved one. Eventually we learn it is as natural as our own breath to give voice to our sadness, even while we place our trust in God for the future.

"Elegy of the Moon"

Tonight, as I look at the moon
My soul cries out for you
The stark contrast of white on endless black
Sharp as have and have not
Tonight, I can't find the way to remember you are with God
Only that you are not with me.

Desiree Woodland ©2011

Close as a sister and brother could be

age eight

Ryan loved being a goalie and played soccer for several years

Team White Sox

Junior year in high school

My heart is glad when I remember our family all together

Our last family vacation spent skiing and snowboarding. We had a blast, and our hearts were knit together one final time before the illness.

One of the last photos of Ryan. He restored this Acura Integra from top to bottom. I am so glad I snapped it.

Chapter Six

MEMORIES

Suicide. The word uttered in the same breath as the precious words, *my son* didn't make sense. I had been hurled into an abyss, dark and unimaginably cold, and I wondered if there was any light on earth left for me. Nothing touches the heart of a mother more than the suffering of her children. What happened to Ryan changed me, forcing a canyon in my soul. Sorrow had created crags and fissures within before unknown.

Memory. In the long weeks and months following Ryan's death I desperately tried to piece together the past. Memories might light the way through this intolerable darkness—but they are memories forever intertwined with a *before* and *after*.

My heart was ragged and torn, and I pined for earlier times when I learned the importance of mothering from my own mother, and then, with the blessing of my two children, from Michelle and Ryan. I began to stitch these earliest memories together with fragile strands of hope so they could begin to mend my heart.

Motherhood is a great blessing and one that I could never take for granted. It speaks of God's unconditional love as He weeps over Jerusalem like a mother who cries when her children are in pain. The journal entries, stories and poems, are mine from the early years to the present, and I included more of Ryan's journal.

What does it mean to be a mother? A woman gives birth, but this does not make her a mother. Conversely, some women who never have children of their own become stand-in mothers for those without a mother-figure. A mother must be strong and courageous as she ventures into the unknown, taking responsibility for precious souls that depend upon her. The most important demand is the ability to love, knowing that she may suffer because of that love. Indeed a mother who loves with absolute abandon and without condition will eventually come to realize that with much love comes much pain.

I have always believed motherhood was the best job in the world, because of my mother's compelling, self-sacrificial example as she reflected God's love with dignity and holiness.

Her sweet love ran deep, but had human limits, as all mothers' love does. Growing up is a difficult process and often leaves scars and emotional baggage despite a parent's best intentions. Thinking they may prevent such damage, parents sometimes try and protect children from trouble, but the ability to deal with difficulty creates individuals with self esteem, who become more capable adults.

Raising six children, along with the worry of managing and caring for not just physical needs, but emotional and spiritual as well, must have been an overwhelming task. But, Mother placed her trust in someone greater than herself, her heavenly Father. She trusted that He would take care of her precious lambs in ways that she could not. This is the legacy she gave us; a picture of the strength of God's love to carry us through life's ups and downs. I could never have guessed how much her example of genuine faith would be a rock for my own life.

We children often tested her patient demeanor, but even when spent and exhausted, she managed to discipline in a way that separated the wrongful act from the child. Once, after a tug-of-war between the three eldest kids, we accidentally broke her favorite teacup, the one that had belonged to her father, and she comforted us with "It's only a thing, girls. Things cannot replace you." Her words soothed our sobs of regret, for we had broken something of value to her. We were given a priceless gift that day, forgiveness freely given and undeserved. She had a way of letting acceptance shine through which made us all stand a little taller.

It was Mother's practical approach and my own experiences in caring for my younger siblings that inspired me to begin babysitting at age 12. I approached my first job with confidence. Of course I could take care of a three day old infant. But, peeking into her crib my courage melted into panic. I had never seen such a small human being. She began to whimper, and soon the whimper quickly turned into a full scream. I was nervous knowing I would now have to pick her up, and soon! In spite of my fears, I gingerly grasped her tiny body which seemed so fragile, and began to rock her back and forth while I hummed a little tune, mostly to calm my own rapidly beating heart. I had watched Mother do this plenty of times. The sounds seemed to soothe her and she quieted.

When she began to cry again I warmed the bottle of milk and placed her tiny head in the crook of my arm. Her rosebud lips closed around the nipple and in a matter of minutes she had consumed the bottle's entire contents. I carefully place her on my shoulder, softly patting her to elicit a burp. When she fell back to sleep, I felt proud because I had not only survived, but thrived.

The promise of the future is birthed in the hearts of children, and I knew I wanted them to be part of my future. The desire to make them a centerpiece of life was an early dream and I hoped one day to have some of my own.

How is the value of mothering measured? The rewards are spiritual with the harvest of love given and reciprocated in our children's very beings. Memories lie dormant in our hearts as time carefully stores them and even if we must dig for them as for hidden treasure, they are surely there.

How we remember, what we remember and why we remember
form the most personal map of our individuality.

Writing and collecting poetry became a way to keep memories of time's passage. Using words, grace painted memories on the canvas of my soul. "After Today" is one such strand of grace.

"After Today"

When you are old I will not have to say "Potty", "Kool-Aid"
I will not have access to your seats; will not take tangles from your hair.
When you are old I will not hold you in my lap
stroke you into the night
give medicine by the teaspoons
Define what "at least" means
explain "America"
When you are old I will take my flesh back
order my days
soak my dreams into my spirit
no longer split by umbilical cries.
When you are, at last, old

I will rest into my life
I will sing
I will be glad
for the days you were young
for the days I am old.

Jain Sherrard

Reading those passionate words evokes deep emotion, and my heart is filled with a sense of having been partners with God in bringing human souls to the planet. Our first child, Michelle, was born in 1978 at the Southwest Maternity Center. "Please, let's don't have any more children," I whispered to my husband even though it had only been a mere 8 hours of labor. Becoming parents for the first time has no equivalent in earthly joys. Michelle opened our eyes to the love of God as no preacher had ever done.

The passage of time changes things and eventually I forgot the pain of childbirth. Wanting another child, Gary and I trusted God for one more, this time a boy, Lord willing. Like Hannah of old I recited, "For this child, I prayed . . . as long as I live he is given to the Lord (I Samuel 1:27, 28)." Ryan Marshall Woodland was born three years after his sister. My husband Gary and sister Sandy were there along with Michelle to watch Ryan's birth. After another short labor he emerged from the warm darkness into his dad's waiting arms. Ryan took his first breath and looked surprised, as if to say, "I wonder why I'm here?" No tears, no crying just a mild, mellow and wonderfully made baby boy with curly hair tinged with red just like his father's! I was struck by his mild nature even then. I looked into his hazel eyes and was transported away from time and space. I knew at that moment that I would do everything in my power to keep him safe. I caressed him and pressed my lips to his wet and swollen head. At nine and half pounds it was hard work for him to enter the world.

Having a boy was an added treasure for my heart. Rocking him, holding him, loving and teaching him, add priceless riches to my inner storehouse.

Ryan, you were a gift and completed the family God had in mind. He knew you before you were born. And He knew every detail about you, your temperament and personality, and what your life would contain. You were loved from the beginning and are loved still. I am ever grateful that He made me your mother and that I had the privilege of watching you grow.

Somehow I sensed there would be only two children in the Woodland family and that I would never again feel life growing within me or experience the joy of giving birth. My journals tell of a strange feeling of grief at the six-week checkup. This mourning was the deepest sadness I had yet encountered. I knew it was part of a universal sorrow that all mothers experience as we prematurely mourn the day when our children will be in their own skins . . . . separate individuals from us. Looking back, I wonder if that sadness was also a foreshadowing of another kind of 'letting go' I would mourn.

There was much joy at the dedication of three month old Ryan to the Lord. In the contemporary Christian tradition, rather than baptism, children are brought before the congregation and prayed over, in essence, given back to the Lord. Parents are prayed for to be good, wise examples of God's love to the child. We proudly took our responsibility for another little one and would do our best to train him, love him and allow ourselves to be knitted together by strands of His grace.

I remember a professional photo taken of Ryan at three months of age sitting next to his sister. Ryan, the baby boy of my dreams, dressed in a baseball suit with the faintest of smiles upon his usually serious face. His sister's chubby toddler hand placed upon his shoulder as if to protect him.

As I ponder this wonderful beginning to his life, I say with God's assurance in my heart that we were the family Ryan needed. I was the mom that Ryan needed, and certainly, Ryan was the son and brother that God knew we all needed.

Life as a mother continued to move forward with the millions of details mothers deal with daily. Experiencing all "the firsts" like crawling, walking, starting school, friendships, how to teach morals and values, the importance of reading and education, and church attendance, all monumental to me. My task was undertaken with gladness and much prayer. I was not always confident that I was doing the right thing, but learned to relax in trust. As with my own mother before me I intended my children would know their worth and value to their parents as well as to God.

Ryan's coming into the world completed our family and immediately we became a foursome. Adult bikes were outfitted with baby and toddler seats respectively. A new tradition was born and we rode to a local restaurant each Saturday morning. Upon waking, Michelle would creep downstairs for the usual cartoons while I nursed Ryan. We'd pull on sweat pants and old tee shirts, and after Gary checked the tire pressure, we'd be on our way. Those Saturday morning breakfasts allowed us time to notice and appreciate one another and time to talk about hopes and dreams for the future.

And the dreams for the future were always bright.

Eventually both kids learned to ride their own bikes. Sometimes we'd ride to the Nature Center near the Rio Grande and walk our bikes through the thick sand left over from days when the river was a mighty force in the Southwest. Michelle and Ryan chattered on about unusual flora or insects they might see.

Like other families, we often had game night. Ryan would go along with any game that Michelle chose. Yahtzee, Monopoly, CandyLand, Chinese Checkers, Hearts or Old Maid were the usual choices. Ryan would bring along his favorite stuffed animals and place them on the floor next to the game. It was their voices we'd hear because Ryan enjoyed pretending they were playing in his place.

I allow myself to be transported into another scene from the past. I see a beautiful blonde head atop a strong sturdy boy running a race with no one in particular. His feet move with a rhythm that only he can hear. "I win!" he shouts at his sister who wasn't in the race. I sense a priceless love between an older sister and her brother. As young children Michelle and Ryan played everything together. She taught him how to play house with dolls as children, how to play school and doctor. He taught her how to play in the mud and get really dirty, how to flip on the bars, and how to do a not so graceful swan dive! Children grow and move on in so many ways, that our minds think that they cannot remember such memories. Indeed, if not for this opportunity to write them here, I would have thought they were gone. They bring healing warmth to my raw heart. Threads of grace.

My tattered journals overflow with other memories and anecdotal notes, as well as excerpts from Ryan's journal the last months of his life.

July 1991
Mother's Journal

O Lord I need your wisdom. Children are so valuable and precious. I treasure the special times with Michelle and Ryan. But it is in only snatches of time. I cannot hold them close for long periods anymore. The hours spent in the rocking chair holding them as babes are long past and the rocking chair sold long ago. But the memories are with me always. I thank you Lord for the memories that record the precious things of life.

The power of language transports me to another dimension. It teaches me to see with eyes of faith into the life beyond while cherishing the life that is now. And the life that I lived as a young mother was indeed to labor with the Creator.

Mother gave me a beautiful poem when Ryan was born that expresses the joy of having a boy in our family. She embellished it with a water-colored picture of a mother rocking her newborn son, and it hangs in Ryan's room . . . even now.

"Polishing Memories"

I have no time to sweep the floor
The piano collects dust like never before.
The wastebasket is full: there are marks on the wall:
The telephone's ringing—can't take any calls.
I'm sitting here rocking my tiny new son,
closing my eyes to the day's work not done.
I know from experience the future becomes past.
These moments are treasures; I want them to last.
Long after he's grown I'll sit in this chair
and feel the soft touch of his baby-fine hair.
I'll rock by this window till the first star appears
polishing the memories of my childbearing years.

Patricia W. Hiscock

We survivors work to keep the light of memory in our lives. Suicide is an ugly word that can overshadow the joy of having known and loved that person. With time and patience we may learn to hold the bad, as well as the cherished good memories of our precious ones, and maybe both at once.

You laughed, cried, played sports, had friendships, and learned to do so many things like taking apart every machine or tool to see how it worked! I remember in karate how proud you were of attaining your first colored belt by breaking a board apart with your kick! I remember how you wanted to save the board for your children to show them what you had accomplished at age 10. As your parents Dad and I wanted to expose you to a variety of experiences like baseball, soccer, gymnastics, and then when you were too cool for these kinds of activities you formed a band and music became your love. Then it was trumpet lessons and after school clubs. You were on your way to becoming a well rounded young person.

January 1992
Mother's Journal

Quality 'minutes' spent with my children. O, God, life moves by so quickly. I wish that wasn't so. A mother must be constantly attuned to these moments that are teachable to impart love . . . moments that hugs and kisses are squeezed into.

Good discipline requires time. From M. Scott Peck's book *The Road Less Traveled*:

"Perceiving in our kids the subtle needs for discipline, taking time to make minor corrections and adjustments, listening to them, responding to them, tightening a little here, loosening a little there, giving them little lectures, little stories, little hugs and kisses, little admonishments, and pats on the back. Children are not blind when they see their parents willing to suffer with them. The feeling of being a valuable person is essential to mental health—it is a direct product of parental love—such a conviction must be gained in childhood; it is extremely difficult to acquire during adulthood. Conversely, when children have learned through the love of parents, it is almost impossible for the vicissitudes of adulthood to destroy their spirit."

That is unless of course the path of their life takes on a dark change—that of mental illness. In Ryan's journals it is clear that he felt unconditional love. I believe this was God's love. He thanked us for loving him since day one. He received our love and gave it back a million times over. He seemed so emotionally grounded that I wondered at the chain of events that led to this kind of ending to his life. If only a mother's love could have saved him from the affliction of mental suffering, he would still be here.

May 1992
Mother's Journal

From a book by Sue Monk Kidd, *Love's Hidden Blessings*, "Make the most of every day. Time does not stand still. One day this hand will wave goodbye while crossing life's brave hill. Of course motherhood has its frustrations and demands. Every worthwhile thing does. Why not accept them instead of dwelling on them? The important thing is to delight in my children now before these moments also become yellowed memories."

I am eternally grateful that I was given time to delight in my children. During their early years, one of our favorite pastimes was reading together. Dark fall and winter evenings we lay on pillows as their Dad read aloud from books like *Chronicles of Narnia, Watership Down, Hafferty the Hamster, Beautiful Joe and The Velveteen Rabbit*. These books contained important life lessons and enduring values. The skin horse in *The Velveteen Rabbit* describes what it means to 'become real.' He says, "We become authentic persons through our willingness to love and be loved, even when it means becoming worn by sacrifice, even when the demands make our faces wrinkled and our joints grow loose."

As a mother I often felt worn by sacrifice and could see evidence of wrinkles when I looked in the mirror. But, no matter, mostly I hoped I was an authentic example of love for my children. I hoped that when the time came to let them go, I would love them enough.

"Only This"
Sometimes
there is only this to do,
Gather the loves in your life
and hold them close
To the lining of the inside
of all that you are.

As they move away
each to their separate worlds,
there is only this to do
See them in their own skins
and note
that to love them
and have that love returned

is after all,
to have the whole
of what you'll ever
long for.

Jain Sherrard

May 1991
Mother's Journal

Tonight there is a brilliant New Mexico sunset. To get a better view Ryan and I decide to climb onto the deck of his swing set/sand box. Mothers cannot always let their children win, so I am first on deck. I hear Ryan's exasperated, "Oh, man!" because the last one up has to recite a poem from memory. He chose one of our favorites called "Sunset" by Lilian Moore. I listen proudly as the words slide off his tongue. Maybe my love of language is beginning to take root!

"Sunset"

There's dazzle in the western sky
Colors spin and run
The pond mouth lies open greedy
for the last rays of setting sun.

Reaching through years, I remember when we sat under that dusky New Mexico sky. Once again I can sense the joy of our connection, and in that moment we were the only people in the world. I believe Ryan felt cherished. God loves each of us in just that way because relationship is the very foundation of Christian faith. The God of the Universe longs for a relationship with His creation and sent His son to earth to reveal Himself to us.

In journals from 1997 I find writing about my development as a mother, teacher and human being. I am just beginning to discern the shape of myself, the person who has been there all along. I see that I could not have hurried the growth. This would have been like planting a seed one evening and expecting it to produce a full plant the next day! I have carved out this life that I am living, but it has not been a product of my own doing. I have needed many people . . . I needed my son.

How could I ever have discerned that Ryan was to become one of my best teachers?

August 2006 after Ryan's death
Mother's Journal

Grief is confusing and paradoxical. This morning when I awoke instead of dread for the day, I was filled with gratitude for the years of laughter and joy that Ryan brought to our lives. He loved making up words, sayings and jokes. I smile when I remember Snowball, a polar bear puppet, he loved to make 'talk', the practical jokes he used to play, the tender, sentimental quality about his love for his mother, the tears and sorrow he felt when he buried any of the many hamsters he had in his life. I remember his crashes in the ditch on his motorcycle, how he wanted to ride his bike to 1st grade with Ben and how nervous I was to let him do it. We laughed when another friend spent the night and rolled out of the loft bed without waking up! But, he did manage to wake up everyone else. These are precious gems stored away forever in my heart.

The letting go that comes with motherhood can only be tolerated in degrees. As Michelle and Ryan grew and influences outside the home expanded their horizons, it was difficult to let go. Letting go of Ryan's physical presence in death has been one of the most painful parts of mothering.

As they moved through the school years, my husband and I faced the same challenges that all parents face. Trust, responsibility, driver's licenses, cars, first jobs, first dates, parties . . .

Watching, with bated breath, our children navigate the treacherous waters of growing up; we parents hope we haven't harmed them in any way. To see them in their own skins, happy and healthy is one of the greatest pleasures of this life.

But the happiness of a young man's life marred by the beginnings of a hidden illness made life especially challenging for Ryan. It added twists and turns that most people take in stride, but for him became utterly important.

Letter to Ryan on his 21st birthday

Dearest Ryan,

As I sit here and ponder how time could have gone by so quickly, I am reminded of the promise you held at your birth. The promise of a mellow child to make a quiet mark on the world . . . this was my first impression of you. Your life has had many unexpected twists and turns, as all fellow sojourners have had. Life is just a series of days held together by the strands of time. What you do with those days is your life's work.

The best wish I can hope for you on this day is to know who you are, to determine who you want to be, and to be true to yourself. I am blessed to be your mom. You have touched my life in so many ways. I am certain and convinced that you *will* find your way through life's journey, though sometimes treacherous, always meaningful and often joyful. We find our way one step at a time.

I love you and am proud to be,
Your mom

Sorrow masquerading as bravery, this letter was written to soothe my spirit with hope for something miraculous to fix the 'unknown something' that hung in the air. But we were already on a rollercoaster slowly making its descent, and within a few years it would take us over the edge. And we would be helpless to stop it.

For the three years before Ryan died, I prayed daily as he struggled to create a life. I prayed he would fulfill his destiny, and I asked God for relationships and companionship. For a wife, purpose and direction, wholeness, and for any mental suffering or turmoil, I asked that he be released. I prayed that he would sense God's presence and that his eyes would be open to the possibilities of this life—not held in bondage to fear, small mindedness, or procrastination. And so I said *Lord, his future is in Your Hands.*

Not really knowing about or believing in mental illness, I was just covering all the bases.

Ryan's Journal

"You are the best mother that ever walked the earth. You loved me unconditionally. You taught me how to read and so many other things I can't even mention. You made me laugh, you held me when I cried, and you kissed my boo-boos, and made them better. I can't even express how much I love you. I loved spending time just you and me. I felt at peace. At home. Just going to the bookstore and getting a coffee. I love you."

"You have always been the most kind, giving parents, and have always put your children's interests ahead of your own. You did your jobs right. This decision has absolutely nothing to do with issues other than my hearing and balance problem. I wish I could continue living with you guys. You are the most wonderful people, and you do not deserve the pain I must inflict on you. I really wish there was another way, but there is not."

Part of our job as parents is to keep our children safe, but it is only an illusion because we do not have that power. We do what is within our human ability, but after that we must trust them to a power greater than ourselves because there are too many things we cannot save them from.

With all the straining towards the future that Ryan tried to do, I think he was never quite able to make that necessary disconnect into the world at large. I remember, as a young boy how he never wanted to leave me: he wouldn't go to preschool (he said he wasn't quite ready), and in elementary school, there was always a special bond. God knew, God knows. A friend wrote on a card after Ryan left: "Somehow you knew that he'd always be with you." These words ring true in my heart today and for always.

"My Boy's Life"

Husky boy-cry awakens my motherhood afresh.
Nine and a half pounds of sweet, pink baby flesh and spirit.
Sweet and innocent sojourner.
Boy in motion, busy with boy-work.
Building forts, riding bikes, playing soccer.
Always time for hugs and kisses,
Sprinkled with a bedtime story or two.

Screeching trumpets honed to perfect pitch,
Head full of dreams—jazz musician, sound engineer, skateboarding pro.
Days of music, girls and cars.
Black engine grease from head to toe lodging in calluses and cracks,
A workman's hands.
The ecstasy in taking apart a car engine, to rebuild it and make it new.
Exquisite look of joy upon his face!

Gentle young man without malice,
No longer at peace in this world.
Fly away home, my son!

Desiree Woodland ©2006

If we are to become fully human we cannot shrink from the work of mourning. Mothers mourn by learning how to live out our days without the child we bore. With no guide book to follow we create a personal grief map for ourselves. But, how will we do it in a way that would make our children proud?

In order to regain some equilibrium and grasp hold of something truer and deeper than the pain, I forced myself to distill it into statements of fact that I was able to hold in my heart. *Fact:* Ryan had more good years than bad. *Fact:* I will always be Ryan's mom—death does not change that. *Fact:* I was the best mother I could be at the time.

The best mother I could be at the time. Could I accept this statement? Five months after Ryan died, in a stupor, I vaguely remember making a plane reservation. I had to get to my daughter. The funeral had not afforded Michelle and I much time together and I desperately needed to know how she was doing, and if she was ok. Would I be able to support Michelle in her grief, when my own heart hurt so badly?

My flight was early so I called her cell phone. No answer. Deciding to wait outside the Sacramento airport I scanned up and down looking for a vehicle I had never seen, and for which I had forgotten to ask the description. Nervously, I peered at the tinted windows of each passing vehicle to see if she was in it. *Please let her find me.*

I watched as some cars circled around the small terminal again and again. Finally a silver truck stopped and the person inside rolled down the window. "Are you hungry? Where should we eat?" her wonderful, familiar voice was like warm honey to my soul. She picked an Asian favorite of hers. The darkness of the restaurant was comforting and being with her a gift. We enjoyed our dinner along with simple conversation. *How have you been? How do you like California? How is your job? What about the dog?* We caught up on some minor details of life, but both of us wanted to talk about Ryan. Pulling into her driveway the porch lights of the houses along the cul-de-sac twinkled against the dark background of the night sky. Their welcoming brightness only served to illumine our loss. I gathered my bags while she opened the front door, and when my feet touched the threshold, emotions held back during dinner came flooding out. My bags dropped to the floor and both of us sank in a heap on the couch. We wrapped our arms around each other tighter than ever before. She laid her head on my shoulder and I stroked her hair wet with tears. Our tears mingled as we cried for all we had lost—for Ryan, for ourselves, for our family, for the future. We sat for hours talking, crying, hugging and talking some more. "Ryan was suffering and we didn't know what to do," she sobbed. "How helpless we all were," "I didn't understand he was mentally ill." "My heart hurts so to learn how much pain he was in."

I hadn't known how deeply to probe into her grief, but needn't have worried, for her words came tumbling out. Minutes turned to hours as we allowed our grief full expression. Neither of us wanted to break the sanctity of what had transpired, but exhaustion was taking over. Just before heading off to bed, she whispered, "I would not be the person I am now without the mother you were, both the good and bad." Tears streamed down the familiar path of my cheeks and soothed me as water upon dry thirsty ground. Her words had forced the tiniest crack in a hard knotted place in my heart. *Thank you, Michelle. Thank you.*

And she had given her loss a voice. It was painful work. Hard, honest work. But, the bonds between us had been strengthened, and although we would each live out our grief in our own way and time, the love and forgiveness of that night would remain forever.

I will always celebrate the love of both of my children. But the bonds between the living and the dead have forced a change because I never knew grief before. She is special in her living, and he in his dying, and through his illness and death he continues to teach our family what it means to live when we think we can't go on.

Chapter Seven

THE WORK OF GRIEF

The journey through grief is for an appointed time.
Ecclesiastes 3: 1, 4

I reach out grasping words left by others so I do not have to travel this unknown path alone. I am a collector of stories, gleaning from the remnants of other's sorrow. I am bereaved: *robbed and torn apart*. Losing my child to mental illness and a violent death cuts to the core and leaves me to languish in desperation. I have become part of a sorrow like no other under heaven, and I feel selfish in my sadness. I grieve for him; I grieve for my lost self.

I was not angry at Ryan for the way he died, but filled with guilt over the mysterious illness that pushed him to it. Isolating himself, his life had become strange and small—he was always around. I mourn the loss of his company and the special bond we shared. Why couldn't I have helped him, I wonder for the umpteenth time?

Intense longings washed over me when I found reminders of the boy he once was, for the man he never became. The toys, the cars, the books, the school papers and artwork carefully saved for a future time when I would show them to Ryan's children, my grandchildren. But now, time stood still.

I never understood the definition of grief before, its *affliction, misery,* and *desolation.* To learn it in this way seemed a cruel joke. Once upon a time my life had seemed so perfect. I was married to the man of my dreams since age eighteen, had two beautiful children, a lovely home, a college education, strong friendships, family and faith. The everyday 'sufferings' like dealing with disappointment or troubles were annoying, but certainly not life changing. But the unspeakable had happened and my life was thrown into a state of panic. Pain was now an irreversible constant and even when its fiery intensity lessened, I would live out the rest of my days without Ryan. This is the pain against which I will measure all subsequent pain. Death hurts like hell.

I found small momentary comforts in *Healing After Loss,* a grief meditation book by Martha Whitmore Hickman. "I know well there is no comfort for this pain of parting, the wound always remains, but one learns to bear the pain, and learns to thank God for what He gave, for the beautiful memories of the past, and the yet more beautiful hope for the future,"

I must periodically empty the overwhelming sorrow of yearning for my missing child. How can I learn to do without his physical presence, this person who was part of my heart, body and soul? If I could forget him, I would not feel grief. But grief, after death, is the price for memory, and learning how to mingle the sorrow of loss with the joy that he was here, the work of grace.

Corinne Chilstrom in *Andrew, You Died Too Soon,* said after her son's death by suicide,

"Grief is chaotic and it dries up the words of prayer. In the long journey of grief how does one pray when there are no words? A major grief is truly a root experience, for one is cut off at the root. One survives, but the new plant will be different."

After eight years she writes that she continues to grieve. She needs to cry her heart out from time to time, and if she doesn't, grief builds up and becomes destructive. Healing is recognizing that nothing will ever be normal again, but there *will* be a new normal.

Grief feels as if you're crawling out of your skin. But I will sit with my grief. Because Ryan's death is important enough to give my grief the time it needs.

"Child of the Living God"

Your true essence is a child of the living God.
No regrets that you were born and lived,
I am grateful for your life . . . a gift from God.
You were a young man with integrity who wrestled so valiantly against the prison your mind had become, mental illness.

You never saw it; we saw it too late, the cure elusive,
But you struggled with all of your strength to beat the progression
of the hearing loss that was your reality . . . until one day you could
struggle no more.

Desiree Woodland ©2006

Ryan's Journal

"I grow tired, weary of the daily cycle of life. It is a joyless process now for me. I wish to relieve my parents of the burden. Sometimes the ear damage seems reparable . . . maybe a hearing aid. But then it hits me, when I don't hear correctly there is no joy in life. Everyday used to be an adventure and thrill no matter if it was work or school. Hearing well made everything fun. Hearing badly makes everything dreary and depressing. My whole spark for life is gone. Sound used to be my life force. It strengthened my soul directly, via, music mostly but everyday sounds also. My brain is wired for sound. Take that away or alter it via hyperacusis and now, loss of clarity and loss of hearing, is too much for me. My soul died that day five years ago when I first got hyperacusis. It continued to progress until my ears totally collapsed and all sounds hurt my ears. I had to wear earplugs constantly. This was extremely devastating to me. My life changed drastically, as my friends can tell you. I wouldn't go anywhere near a loud party, but I managed to have somewhat of a social life. I also managed to keep working."

"But, recently I used an antibiotic known to cause your hearing to deteriorate. Instantly, I noticed that my tinnitus, which was mild and bearable, became louder. My hearing became distorted and awful sounding. I was suffering from ototoxicity, which is known to cause changes in hearing quality. So basically I am left with distorted hearing but not much of a change in my audiogram. This causes everyone around me to think I'm making up the whole thing. And the hearing continues to get worse."

"I couldn't live without my hearing. I couldn't be happy without my good hearing. If I'm not happy, and I can't function, I'm just a burden. I'm sorry Mom and Dad and Michelle. I'm so weak. I couldn't handle it anymore. I know some people with the same exact problems as me don't react like this. I don't know why I couldn't just accept it and live on. Too afraid, too weak. Mostly I just wish I could make you guys happy again."

"I'm so sorry. Please don't hate me. I only wanted to stop all of this pain. Stop the pain. I've never experienced suffering like this before and I wanted it to be over. I'm sorry. I just didn't see me ever having a normal life again. Just existence, which is not the same. I don't want to die, but I saw no other alternative. Hearing well and enjoying music were among my highest priorities. Without music, I got very depressed. No more music. I could not imagine living in a world like that for the rest of my life. I just can't deal with messed up hearing. I can't deal with the fear of the unknown. I'm trying to explain my situation to the best of my ability, so you guys won't wonder why. But, I don't think any explanation will really make it ok. I'm so sorry you guys. I know it sounds selfish and I'm so sorry. My life is over. Every word I write make makes my depraved mental condition more apparent. I wrote as much as I could so you guys would have something to go on, and maybe have some closure and some answers."

Grief washes over me in that place between sleeping and waking. And in spite of what I believe, often feels like a nightmare. If I allow grief to do its work, might it reveal how to reconcile Ryan's suffering with life going forward? A brave declaration, but the wound is wont to reopen when I see someone he knew before he got sick or go somewhere he used to love. His life never matured or grew into fullness. I feel suffocated and smothered. I cry so easily—when will this be over?

The words of Dietrich Bonhoffer bring comfort,

> "Nothing can fill the gap when we are away from those we love, and it would be wrong to try and find anything. We must simply hold out and win through. That sounds hard at first, but at the same time it is a great consolation, since leaving the gap unfilled preserves the bond between us. It is nonsense to say that God fills the gap; he does not fill it, but keeps it empty so that our communion with another may be kept alive, even at the cost of pain."

I cannot always feel Ryan in my heart and so I imagine kissing his cheek and his strong arms hugging me tight. I miss him. Condemnation hangs heavy. The litany of *If only; what if; I should have known*, ring in my head.

When grief is new, it is possible to entertain these kinds of thoughts, even to examine the truth of them. But as I stumble through, it becomes apparent that what is, is. What a hard saying. I push it away and yet, I must accept that what has happened did not take God by surprise. Ryan died, God knew, and nothing could have prevented it. Suicide is not predictable because there is never just one cause. But even if I had known all the signs and symptoms, would it have made a difference? We overestimate our influence over another person when we think we are that powerful. If love alone could have saved him, he would still be alive. My love was deep while my knowledge of mental illness was nil.

The nature of Ryan's illness was a mystery. Why didn't he respond to anti-psychotic drugs? The delusion was strong, stronger than Ryan's willpower, stronger than the drugs, stronger than a parent's love, but not stronger than God's love. I read somewhere that if someone wants to commit suicide they will find a way to end their pain. I must rest in this. What terrible words to rest in, but I receive comfort knowing that Ryan is now at peace. I love him and would not ask that he come back to suffer again.

Bits and pieces of grief spilled onto paper turning into desperate words and questions; words to sort through the confusion and desolation of what had happened. If more people understood mental illness and suicide the world would be so much better off. Might Ryan's suffering change something in the world? O God please let it be so; don't let his illness and death be wasted.

All entries 2006 are after Ryan's death
Mother's Journal

Each day I cry out, sobbing until my heart hurts, but it hurts for me. I try to rest in the idea that you are at peace and finally free. I am left to make my life honorable to God without you in it. Dusk fades into night and I strain to see your face. Each day upon awakening, the prospect of living my days without you clouds my heart and mind. I stare at your picture, missing you. Feelings come unbidden. When I cry the grief built up inside empties out. This is how I make room in my heart for whatever God has for my future. Love doesn't end, but expands. I will work with God towards a future that keeps room for you always in my heart, but also for the meaning and purpose that your death will bring to my life. Even so, grief is an amputation of a bit of my soul. I will grieve until I am able to let it go.

What does it mean to let go of grief? Who would I be without this last strong bond to my son? It doesn't mean I love Ryan any less, does it? Corrine Chilstrom feels this awkward ambiguity when she writes:

"Intense grief is an unwelcome experience; it can evoke feelings of helplessness, fear, guilt, and defeat. It is not surprising that we attempt to minimize it. Bereavement is not an easy or a speedy task. In fact, it takes far more courage to be open to the work of mourning, to be willing to experience one's own vulnerability and actually walk among the sufferers than it does to erect emotional armor around one's heart and remain forever hidden behind its protective barricades. The painful work of mourning is essential to the preservation of rich and meaningful existence. The unmourned loss can haunt one's life and cause bitter sadness. Anything lost must be accepted and mourned before it is possible to honor a loved memory and begin a new chapter of life. If the Gospel is to heal us we can't hide grief under a bushel."

In death I am born. Hopi

Finding my way back from Ryan's death is long and hard, but I believe possible. There are no prescriptive rules, no guidebook to follow. Oh, if only there were. To become a survivor I must find ways to transcend the suicide. *Please God, help me to order my days, soak new dreams into my spirit, touched by the sweetness of Ryan.* I didn't choose for Ryan to die, but I must now choose the attitude and direction my life will take because of it. I sense Ryan whisper to me that he isn't gone, but only changed locations. Isn't this after all what I believe about our lives on this earth?

One has to face fear or forever run from it. Crow

2006
Mother's Journal

I am fighting for my life. The pain is almost intolerable, as it has been the past two days. God, are you here, even in this pain? I believe the echoes of God are everywhere . . . there is longing in the human soul for things to be put right. That is where the cross of Jesus meets me, in this pain. This knowledge does not stop the thought of how hard this fight is going to be and it does not prevent me from wanting to give up. Oh, how Ryan fought . . . for as long and hard as he could. Why was there no help this side of heaven? This is an unanswerable question. I know this and yet I persist. I am becoming obsessive/compulsive over Ryan.

What a struggle it is to live life with meaning or purpose. I know it will come, but how to return to a world that doesn't seem to matter anymore? Things seem so unimportant. The empty, lonely isolation I feel even when with others is confusing. I am in turmoil about how to proceed with my life. I am come face to face with fears, insecurities and old wounds that were only covered up before, but now are raw and exposed.

2006
Mother's Journal

September rolls back around for time stops for no one, not even for a grieving mother. So, I am back to work part-time, and each day I rise to thoughts of *I can't do this.* Each day I awake with flashbacks of Ryan. And each day I force myself to practice a thought-stopping technique so I can live the day as I should. I am learning to replace the sad, tormented vision of Ryan with the reality of his freedom. Love must let go. Love must realize that it is not the welfare of the lover, but of the loved one that counts. God did not promise that we would be happy, but that we would know His love. Ryan was a tortured young man, and as much as I miss him, I must let go.

Love always believes the best, love never fails, and it never fades
out or comes to an end.
I Corinthians 13

Fall is in the air, and I receive no pleasure as its splendid show of golden-leaved trees begins its yearly drama. Today I attended the Suicide Survivor's Support group. We talked about the process of grief and its cyclic nature. It was reinforced that grief cannot be hurried; we must move with it. We practiced a technique called *mindful meditation* where we are quiet with God and don't allow our thoughts to wander from the good to the bad or the neutral, just gently bring them back to focus on your breath. This idea has been practiced for thousands of years by many cultures and religions. It was very helpful today. I make a mental note to practice this one more regularly.

2006
Mother's Journal

Time demands more of me than I can bear. Grief takes a circuitous route rising and falling in its intensity. When it returns it interrupts the feeling that I am making progress on this path. We want the quick, easy and cheap route. If we are to take the pain of our loss and let it become the fertile soil of the future then we cannot shrink from its lessons. We want to push away the pain that threatens to engulf us because it makes us question our purpose. But what we need for life is to sit with the magnitude of what has happened. Sometimes we try to bury these emotions but they reside within our psyche and will stay, waiting to be dealt with. Unfulfilled lives, unmet goals and dissatisfaction are the fruit of burial. If I ever hope to have the dignity of a life well lived, making an honorable and satisfying life I must learn to live differently. The melancholy ache of facing life without Ryan is an ever present companion. In spite of returning to part time work and the purpose I am trying to find once again, I often feel empty. It is so hard; and yet I know I must press on toward the prize of the knowledge I will glean about myself. I will take up my cross and follow You, Lord.

Grief is dark. In its wake, I hold tightly to strong wise words that others give me. "Grace," my brother Matthew ministered, "for each day and for a lifetime of need." For nine months I carried Ryan in the dark safety of my womb. And then, kicking, pushing and fighting he came forth into the world. Beautiful miracle of life.

In his final nine months, he lived with deadly thoughts incubating and pulsing through his brain. He was fighting for his life, even as the illness fought to extinguish it. But to hold this awful reality in my heart, I must hold onto another deeper truth. The love I have for Ryan abides through the veil that separates me from him, for it is only a temporary separation. "What is seen is temporary but what is unseen is eternal." (2 Cor. 4:18). Beautiful miracle of life.

Grief is not an affliction to be treated, a crisis to be resolved, closure to be had or an experience to be overcome. Rather, we learn to integrate and reconcile the loss. We must befriend our grief and its effects. One of the life-long effects of grief is missing the warm, living, breathing presence of our loved one. We long to touch them, to breathe in their smell, but we can only hold them in our heart. Rituals can be a tangible way to be *present* as we hold them, if only for a brief moment. Gary and I have created rituals that fill us with the sacred sense of both life and death. They give us a semblance of peace and tie us to Ryan in ways not seen by others, and make meaning when we otherwise cannot sense any.

On the first anniversary of Ryan's death, we gathered with friends and family at the cemetery. Mom and Dad were the first to arrive, with Dad holding Mom's elbow. Her once graceful walk had changed to the Alzheimer's shuffle and both struggled to get to the folding chairs in the front row. After I gently helped her into the first chair, she looked up with her perpetual smile. I hugged her and choked on tears because she didn't know why she had come. This day of remembrance, forever etched on my soul, was a mystery to her.

Standing near Ryan's niche, in solemn meditation I struggled to remember why I thought it was important to gather with everyone today. It's too hard, I thought. I don't feel any comfort being here. But, as the small seating area filled in with the most precious people in the world, I gave in to the emotions I had bottled up throughout the day. It was safe to cry. These people loved me and my family and understood the importance of memory and ritual because for Gary, Michelle and me this was how it would always be.

My brother Matthew began the service with tears and a quaking voice and quoted from Job, "When all that Job loved in this world was taken from him and he still trusted God—he still **hoped** in God, it proved that God was more precious than all that Job loved in the world." Looking at Gary and me, he said, "Through your quiet perseverance you have made Christ look more precious in my sight." How was it possible to display a quiet perseverance when we felt so sad?

The service ended with a circle of love, prayers, wishes and tears. Grateful for these strands that connected our lives to family and friends, I hugged everyone tightly, awed by the power of love that reached into our hearts and pulled us closer to eternity.

For Ryan's birthday, Gary and I released balloons equal to his age. For this first birthday without him there were 25 balloons. His sister Michelle had called early that morning. "I am thinking of him, too," she sobbed. "One balloon is from me." We released each balloon one by one, until the sky over the cemetery was dotted with green balloons. Through tears we watched them rise, eventually disappearing into the deep blue New Mexico sky framed by pure white clouds. Beauty rising from ashes. The people buried here are no longer here—only their bodies, which is not the same.

Are we living in the past trying to keep Ryan's memory alive? Sometimes I wonder if others may think so, but no one who has not lost a child can understand the need these rituals fulfill to help us to deal with the future. As human beings we create ritual and story in order to make sense of our day-to-day lives.

2006
Mother's Journal

Again, today the future looms unending. Ryan didn't know how long we would actively deal with his death, but it is not to be gotten through quickly. Not only is it the initial passing of time, but also the day-to-day pushing through of the future. Getting up each morning and acting like life has meaning but not feeling it. It is a daily struggle to accept this awful thing. Can I accept the fact that Ryan is no longer on this earth? I have no choice. There are vast differences between what I want and what I need. The gap is a chasm.

> *We've got to take reality as it comes to us; there's no good jabbering about what it ought to be like or what we'd have expected it to be like. Our universe contains much that is obviously meaningless, but contains creatures like ourselves who know that it's bad and meaningless. If the whole universe has no meaning: we should never have found out that it has no meaning.*
>
> C.S. Lewis

As much as it felt that time had stopped, it marched on. Time does continue, but its face had changed. Not the deep soul matter of Ryan's leaving, but the intensity of its sharpest edges. I try to face it, make it mine until I can breathe again. Bit by bit, perhaps year by year, I will learn to see joy, color and purpose again. I need to open my hands to life, but I don't want to. Not yet. I know that eventually I must, because there is nothing that can bring Ryan back and if I only grudgingly accept, I will live my life emotionally crippled by his death. Can I trust that God is sovereign over the earth? That He is bigger than I am and there is hope for us all?

Hope is essential to existence. With hope, we can face what life has in store, but without it we are bankrupt. My heart had been numb for so long, and I missed the physical sensation of its warmth. A source of such hope was the birth of my niece's son. On that lovely day in 2009, I was privileged to hold my tiny hours-old grand nephew. Unexpectedly I felt hope's gentle presence while I breathed in the promise of this new life. Sobs welled up and tears rolled down my cheeks because here in my arms was another boy named Ryan. How marvelous. I believed in hope when I looked into the eyes of this precious baby with a name as big as my heart.

What does it mean to hope in God? Do I really mean that I will take all from His hand? Or just the good stuff? Or what I perceive to be the good stuff? Humans have very little control over some things in life. Accepting our powerlessness to effect change in anyone and that sometimes bad things happen that cannot be prevented is a painful reality.

I was not prepared to deal with mental illness, but even more unprepared to deal with Ryan's death. Nothing I had done had made a difference. Even after prayer it made no difference. When this happens what will we as believers believe about God? Are we able to say with gratitude that He is God and we are not? I wanted to believe again the words from Colossians: *that in Him all things were created, in heaven and on earth, things seen and things unseen, all things were created and exist through Him and in and for Him.* Colossians 1:16.

Chapter Eight

BELIEF

Death is real and it is unpleasant, painful and cruel.
Any philosophy or religion that does not have a
positive answer to the reality of death is inadequate
to meet the needs of humanity.

Derek Prince

I wrestled with God, desperately wanting belief to hold me once again. I didn't know if I could find answers, but I needed to sense there was still a foundation upon which to base my life. And I needed hope there would be a balm to soothe the scorching pain of despair that burned in my brain.

June 2006
Mother's Journal

I hate this world that includes so much pain, and no easy answers to address such pain. I cry. I yell. I scream. Emotions are powerful reminders of my humanity. They should not be allowed to rule me, but that's easy to say, harder to practice. How can faith in God's goodness be manifest in the evil of mental illness? Ryan, your mind led you to believe a lie about your ears. Your emotions /mind took over so gradually until you could not discern the truth. It is hard to let the pain go because I have wanted to punish myself by reliving yours, because of my inability to recognize the signs of mental illness, and even if I had, I did not want to admit it. I continued to move forward in my life while you were slowly being eaten up by an illness I could not name. I mourned for you when you let go of another dream, but I didn't know that I was only letting you lose yourself. Letting you? Are these words too strong for what I did not do? Doctors have said that the signs of schizophrenia are almost imperceptible to family members as the disease is taking hold. That is the truth. I saw you let go of jobs, dreams of going to school, music, and skateboarding. All the while you said you didn't like them anymore and they didn't matter in your life, and besides everything was getting too loud and painful for your ears. In your own journals you said you gave up friendships for the sake of your ears. How sad. If treatment is begun early enough could it possibly keep the disease from progressing? How this shreds my heart. I can't be responsible for what I could not see. And who's to say that it would have worked for you? Who can help me now? I am wallowing in self-pity. I only know for certain that I loved you through all of it. Thinking about how your personality changed gradually through the years should have alerted me to something terribly wrong. Why didn't it? Why didn't God let me know?

Could faith light the way through this intolerable darkness? Faith is part of our lives whether we admit it or not. It takes faith to sit on a chair and hope it will hold our weight. It takes faith to drop off a child at school and expect they will be waiting for you at the end of the day. It takes faith to cross a street hoping there is not a speeding drunken driver around the bend. And it takes faith to believe that God has a purpose and plan, which may never be understood, in your child's mental illness and suicide. When we have done all that we know to do and it doesn't make a difference, where will we go to find relief for our souls? What will we believe about God? Will we still believe? The thought of facing the rest of my life without Ryan's physical presence seemed interminable. Sometimes even just one day seemed too long.

> "In a world where there is no room for
> doubt, or ambiguity, or questioning there is
> no room for genuine faith." Alan Jones

As humans, the question of God's existence and/or His goodness haunts us after a tragedy of life-changing proportions. It was of utmost importance that I settle the constant attacks in my mind about the goodness of God. I felt compelled to continue on in the faith and reason walk that I began so long ago, despite deep doubts that had arisen. I had come to faith in Jesus long ago and been a regular part of the church for over thirty years. Being a Christian had shaped my life; I had known no other way to live. Until now, I had not known the significance and importance of Christians being thinking people who ponder hard ethical questions about life and death without fear of the answers. I had always had a pat answer ready for any trial. But when the mysteries of death seemed to yield none, rather than giving up on belief, I reached out into the blackness of night to grab hold of someone bigger than myself to find God.

Not the god who answered every prayer, who always gave me what I wanted and who always delivered me or my family from suffering, as I had once believed. I struggled for faith so that I could hope to understand what the Christian life truly meant, even if that meant going back to the basics of believing in God or not. So I began to study one of the great Christian thinkers and apologists of the 20th century, C.S. Lewis. For many years, Lewis was an avowed atheist. Surely in his writings I could find the balm of God's grace for my troubled soul. I needed to hear from the depths of a man who at one time didn't believe in God and had used his reason to justify his lack of belief. But then using that very same reasoning, he came to faith in God the Creator. He states his reasoning for not, at first, believing in God.

> "Look at the universe we live in. By far the greatest part of it consists of empty space, completely dark and unimaginably cold. The bodies which move in this space itself are so few and so small in comparison with the space itself that even if every one of them were known to be inhabited as full as it could hold with perfectly happy creatures, it would still be difficult to believe that life and happiness were more than a by-product of the power that made the universe. It is so arranged that all the forms of it can only survive by preying on one another. It is consciousness attended with pain."

Lewis painted such a dismal picture of life, and it was such a dismal thing to read after the death of my son. But, I wanted to get to the heart of the matter. I had to begin to understand what I had not understood before about basic belief. He used reason as well as faith to come to the Creator, and then further coming to faith in Christianity. Perhaps here was a faint glimmer of light to satisfy my mind and begin to melt the winter from my soul.

Two other books by him became very important on my quest: *The Problem of Pain*, written before the death of his wife and *A Grief Observed*, written afterwards. Both look at grief, pain, suffering, death, and the question of God's existence.

Lewis's philosophy and writings often contain very complex ideas, so I read and reread his words trying to understand the depth of his weighty perspectives. Faith had never been such a struggle before, there had been no need for lengthy questions, or complicated explanations. It just was.

Somehow I had bypassed the "trials and tribulations" part of this earthly existence. God and I had a good thing going. I prayed, He answered and I said thank you. But now, I was forced to examine carefully what I had to lose or gain by believing in the God of my childhood. Summarizing Lewis's thoughts, I wrote that anthropologists have said religion is an invention that answers the unanswerable questions of existence. Apart from God then, if the world is only "survival of the fittest" and only the strong survive, why do we wonder at the evil that is present in the world and wish for goodness? Where does this idea of *goodness* originate? If there is a God, how did we ever come to attribute goodness to Him?

What was the basis for faith, and if my faith was to survive, I had to ask something I had never before needed to ask. Could God be trusted?

The examination began, for Lewis, with early man. He posed the question that since early man was primarily concerned with survival, how did the fear of animals crouched at his campfire compare with something that he calls *numinous* awe and a sense of wonder, which was separate from the fear? He says, "The spectacle of the universe as revealed by experience can never have been the ground of religion. Furthermore it makes sense that man would be afraid of the saber-toothed tiger at his campfire, which can be seen and heard. But, this awe that has long been expressed in songs, poems or other art forms, where does this intangible idea come from? When man passes from physical fear to dread and awe, he makes a sheer jump, and apprehends something which could never be given, as danger is given, by the physical facts and logical deductions from them."

To Lewis morality is another jump. This is the sense that one "ought" or "ought not" to do things. "Moralities among men may differ," he continues, "but they all prescribe behavior that men ought to practice and don't." According to him the next strand in religious development is when the numinous awe and the moral code come together in a power greater than themselves. This final strand of religious development from Lewis's perspective is the historical event of Jesus' birth. This is the Man who claimed to be "the Something which is at once the awful haunter of nature and the source of moral law." My quest has led me here, and I say with Lewis, that ultimately perceiving a suffering world, and being assured, on quite different grounds, that God is good—how am I to conceive goodness and suffering without contradiction?

> "The problem of reconciling human suffering with the existence of a God Who loves, is only insoluble so long as we attach a trivial meaning to the word 'love' and look on man as if he were the center of things. Man is not the center. God does not exist for the sake of man. Man does not exist for his own sake. Thou hast created all things and for Thy pleasure they are created."

"We were not made primarily that we may love God, but that God may love us," said George MacDonald as quoted by C.S. Lewis in *The Problem of Pain*. God Himself knows suffering, and He suffers with us. Even nature, the Bible says, groans for the earth to be renewed. The Bible teaches that this life is not all there is, and that Jesus went to prepare a place for us in heaven. (Romans 8:19 and John 14:21) Lewis was greatly influenced in the Christian faith after reading George MacDonald's writings.

Heaven had always been something I confessed belief in, but never had reason to question before. But now, I had to know if I believed. Most people seemed to, but what was the basis for their belief? I examined and compared the words of the Bible with the words of scholars, as well as myths from other cultures. There are fascinating stories about life after death from the ancient Babylonians, Egyptians, Indians, Asians, Native peoples, the Jews and the Christians. The idea of resurrection is present in many myths and in nature itself.

Lewis' argument of *numinous awe* speaks peace into my soul about God's existence as Creator. John Eldredge, another Christian apologist, writes in *Divine Romance* about our human longings, that he says, point to God. "Someone or Something has romanced us with long summer days and crickets chirping, pastel sunsets, snowcapped mountains, bright autumn leaves and crisp fires; Someone telling us they are leaving us a promise that they will return. This promise unearths our longings for adventure and desire for intimacy. These things can, in an unguarded moment, bring us to our knees, with longing for this Someone who is lost, Someone that only our heart recognizes."

When loss touches us so deeply we wonder what we will keep. Which beliefs still make sense? And we wonder if we can really know? I want to keep the belief of heaven. Nothing else will satisfy. There are glimpses and longings, which seem to be imbedded in our very souls, if we are not too proud or grown up to admit them.

Heaven is in the feeling or sense of wanting your mama to tuck you in. I remember as a little girl that mom would 'tuck in' all of her kids. If I ever had to get up, for water or the bathroom, it would undo that sensation of safety. She would perform the ritual over again so I could fall asleep. Yes, I outgrew it, but I think that inside every adult there is a still a small child who wants its mom.

I felt the same longing in a Beethoven symphony. I have also known it in the pain and work of a mother who at long last looks upon her baby, the fruit of her labor. Heaven calls us through the changing of seasons, the sun glinting off new fallen snow, the smell of a fire and the giggle of a child's pure enjoyment. In my New Mexico home I feel a nostalgic ache each fall as the cranes fly south for the winter. The gray sky scattered with small clouds brings a lonely feeling which hangs in the air and speaks to something deeper, something universal. I ask why God would have put such longings in us that cannot be completely fulfilled. Surely there must be a place, another world where all of our deepest, unutterable feelings will find their fulfillment.

The words in Ryan's final letter, "We will see each other again", bring no small comfort. He expressed simple faith in another world without pain where all the pieces of the puzzle would finally make sense. I ponder this treasure in my heart.

We are joined with a bond that is eternal and unbreakable, untouchable by illness or death. This world is not our home; these bodies are only temporary houses for our spirits while on this earth. It is the expectation of permanence that causes us pain. And so we look forward with the expectation of our own Home going. Ryan has made us all long for heaven in a new way.

Further in *The Problem of Pain*, C.S. Lewis said, "Heaven will solve our problems, but not I think, by showing us subtle reconciliations between all our apparently contradictory notions. The notions will all be knocked from under our feet. We shall see that there never was any problem. And more than once that impression which I can't describe except by saying that it's like the sound of a chuckle in the darkness—the sense that some shattering and disarming simplicity is the real answer."

Another writer who questioned his belief system after tragedy struck his child was John Gunther. He wrote of his experience in a memoir called *Death Be Not Proud*. His son, John Jr. was diagnosed with brain cancer in 1946 when technology was in its infancy regarding brain surgery or cancer treatment. I have found solidarity with John and Frances Gunther, and the depths to which they cherished their beloved son, John, age 17.

Frances wrote short pieces sprinkled throughout the book. Here, she writes about death, "The impending death of one's child raises many questions in one's mind, heart and soul. It raises all the infinite questions that seem to end with another question. What is the meaning of life? What is the relationship of life to death? Yet, at the end of them all, when one has put away all the books, and all the words, when one is alone with oneself, when one is alone with God, what is in one's heart? Each condolence runs a single theme: sympathy with us in facing a mysterious stroke of God's will, which must also be a part of some great plan beyond our mortal ken (sic), perhaps sparing him or us greater pain or loss."

Along with Frances, I asked what was in my heart. My heart was bruised and sore, and it carried a bitter sweetness I had never known. I questioned what I was made of, even as I stumbled towards the future with hope that I would arrive at some place of resolve with peace and purpose.

Endurance through suffering. This powerful theme resounds throughout Viktor Frankl's book, *Man's Search for Meaning*, and my seeking hungry heart welcomed its nourishment. Published after WWII, it tells of his horrendous experiences in a Nazi concentration camp and the ways in which people dealt with their survival and the very real possibility of their deaths. As a clinical psychologist he tells his own story as well as the stories of the people he met and the difficult struggle to maintain dignity in the midst of dehumanizing conditions. I marvel at the strength of people to endure and wonder if I have this strength. He observed that those who had a purpose for enduring were able to do so.

August 2006
Mother's Journal

The cross is for our unbelief, our not following of God, our pain and suffering in this life. God promises He will complete and finish what He has begun. It was no accident you were born, it was no will of man. God foreordained that you would be born, live your life with Dad and I as your parents, Michelle as your sister, and you as a happy person with a full life ahead of you-until the mental illness came. But God was not surprised by it and whether I did or did not do everything right, God was still with us, daily with us, in the ups and downs of trying to figure out what was happening to you. And when you were actually diagnosed and we were all in shock and disbelief, God was there, even in the doctors' and nurses' care.

Frankl asserted that the difference between those who survived and those who didn't was having a purpose larger than themselves. Man's freedom is not unrestricted and it is not freedom *from* conditions, but freedom to take a stand *toward* the conditions. Out of these experiences he developed a psychological method called logotherapy. It uses the power of language, storytelling and logic (logos) to help people come to terms with trauma in their lives and recognize meaning for themselves in their tragedies. After all, sometimes all I have are words. But I will keep writing until I find some meaning in this suffering. Suffering is so powerful, it is one of the main reasons people use to disavow a belief in God.

But suffering itself, says Frankl, can be an analogy for the existence of God. I ruminate over this; meditate upon its importance to this journey. Speaking to a class of psychology students he posits the question of an ape's suffering as it is repeatedly punctured to supply the blood necessary to develop a polio serum. He asks, "Will this ape ever be able to understand the meaning of its suffering?" Of course the students answer that with its limited intelligence it could not enter into man's world of suffering. "Well, then what about man? Is it not possible that the human world is more than a terminal point in the evolution of the cosmos? Is it not conceivable that there is still another dimension, a world beyond man's world, a world in which the question of an ultimate meaning of human suffering would find an answer?" *Yes,* I answer. *Yes.*

This is our humanity. I cried out to God, I moaned for answers to unanswerable questions, and struggled to trust God for what I knew couldn't be seen or known. It used to be easy to pray. But my faith had been shattered and my emotions strangled, twisted and broken. It was an act of sheer determination to come before God's throne, but my heart would go nowhere else.

I was unable to put the whole of the suffering of humanity into perspective with my own sorrow. I mourned for Ryan. I wrapped myself up in the sadness of him. Confusion, not clear purpose threatened to overcome me. But my heart kept turning towards the Cross. Through its power I hoped I would find a way to live with Ryan's death and face my own inadequacies, fears, and worries for the future.

Can I truly face the future without a piece of my heart? I need solid metaphors for what has happened. I am derailed, how to get back on track? I am drowning; I need life support and a way to get back to land. I am lost, with no map and no destination. Improvise; make it up as I go along. Reinvent myself; banish the fear of becoming someone different. Unpacked baggage; I will have to keep dragging it up the steps of life's journey until I decide to unpack it and put it away.

My quest continued with Joan Didion's book *The Year of Magical Thinking*. She wrote about her husband's death at age 54 and the simultaneous hospitalization of her grown daughter from sepsis. She struggled to come to terms with both life-changing events by writing. I too find I can clarify my thinking and beliefs by writing. Didion said, "I felt no hope in the future. Yet, I professed it in words." I also have felt no hope or faith for the future. Yet I professed my eternal hope in words and prayers, even while not feeling any of it. When death touches you in the deepest most sacred places of the heart, the immensity of it is overwhelming. Pain makes its voice heard through physiological and psychological ways. She continues, "A single person is missing to you and the whole world seems empty."

My mind could not conceive how I would keep living and dealing with the everyday, mundane and sometimes meaningless duties of life. Is time the answer? Time heals all wounds don't they say? Time is indeed part of healing but only because each person heals in his or her own way and timetable. Time alone is not the healer, but it is the willingness and courage to face the pain and search for its inevitable messages to us that heals. One message forged through my pain was, *what I bring out into the light loses its power over me, even if never completely.* I am drawn to learn all I can about mental illness because I am haunted by the memory of how easily I *saw* Ryan without ever really *seeing the cause* of his pain as biological, with a psychological root.

The last line of Didion's book says, "No eye was on the sparrow and no one was watching me." It struck me as sad to end a book about death with no hope but what this present world offers. The line is in reference to Jesus' words from Matthew 10: 28-31, "Are not two little sparrows sold for a penny? And yet not one of them will fall to the ground without your Father's leave and notice. But even the very hairs of your head are numbered. Fear not then; you are of more value than many sparrows."

Ah, yes, the sparrows. How many times had I quoted this verse to remember my value to God, even the eternal value of all human beings?

Yes, the very hairs on Ryan's head *were* numbered. God knew Ryan inside and out and yet he became ill and died. The illness Ryan suffered was of such intensity that he was no longer free. How dare I ask that he return to earth to suffer further? In spite of this, I believe that Jesus was with Ryan in all of his torment. But there are limits to what humans can endure.

Those deep yearnings that catch us by surprise, can they really be telling us something truer about life than all the pain? From where does that knowing come? If from God, can we choose to believe Him when He says He will never forsake us even when it looks like evil has won? If I am ever to live with meaning again, I must learn to place my trust and hope in the fact that God is God and I am not. Faith is inevitable for my existence.

The brain is the chief organ of belief. Death is an experience of consciousness; surely it is an enlarged consciousness of more inclusive vision than we know here. Love binds me to my dead son with stretchable not breakable bonds. I cannot deny the pain of separation and the understanding of *not knowing*. But, like the apostle Paul in the book of Hebrews, I say, "Faith is the assurance of things hoped for and the conviction of things not seen." What we can be sure of from our own experience and the experiences of others is that more is going on in the universe that what we can experience with our five senses.

Annie Dillard said, "We wake, if ever we wake at all, to mystery." Let me wake to mystery and be all right with knowing there is not always a resolution. Is it possible that our lives can actually make sense even when we don't understand? Both the good and the bad? Can I let Ryan go into the hands of the very One Who created him? Trusting that the pain Ryan endured was not out of God's will and God did not abandon him in the dark nights of confusion?

There are no easy answers to questions like these, but I could not abandon God's presence in my life, in spite of the agony of dealing with Ryan's illness and death. Everything I have and everything I will ever have are gifts from Him. Pascal said in the *Pensees* 418: "I have gained in this life by following Him and with each step I have seen so great a certainty of gain that I have 'wagered' for something certain and infinite, for which I have given nothing."

Thus I must roll up my sleeves and get to work: God's will doesn't always look spiritual because there is a *real* quality to life when we walk with Him. It is not outside of the work-a-day world, but right in the midst of it. It is not in pie-in-the-sky, nothing-bad-can-ever-touch-me-if-I'm-God's-will, but walking the thorn way in Jesus' footsteps. Rather than ignoring or running away from our lives we choose to love whether or not we feel like it, we choose belief whether we feel like it or not. God is not in a hurry to make us what He had in mind when He created us. He will take as long as it takes. While in this desert time of life I have wanted to run away, but instead I must run to God and be obedient. God will go to great lengths to keep us in His will. I belong to God and whether I live or die, I belong to Him and He knows the purpose and plan for my life.

For now, I only see *through a glass darkly but then I shall see face to face.* I came to the abyss of existential darkness and knew I couldn't live without hope. I felt alone grasping at what it means to live, but without God, I could find no meaning in existence.

I reasoned out my faith as far as reason could reach and at the end of it, faith was waiting for me. Not a blind faith that made stabs at God in the dark or a faith that gave me all I thought my heart desired, but a faith that trusted in Him even when I could not make any sense of life, a faith beyond words.

One day I will see and understand the awesome power of God and the perfect plan He made for our lives. *Jesus, please let me see you as the incredible and awesome Creator who is helping me find my way back from this dark abyss. You are my Burden Bearer. I cannot bear the weight of this any longer. You were not surprised by Ryan's death. Release me from the strength of the guilt that tries to strangle my heart. Help my thinking to align with what I believe. I give it all to you, the heaviness, the depression, the worry, the blame, the "should haves" and rest in you. In Psalms 51:8, Ecclesiastes 3:1, Isaiah 26:3, John10: 11, 14 and John 16:3, I find I can frame more of my beliefs. I believe God is still on the throne. He is sovereign in a world that seems out of control. He knows each of us and longs to carry us through the pain. He has always had a plan and known the length and hours of each of our days on this earth. He will be glorified in Ryan's death and his parents' grieving. He doesn't make mistakes, and He knew Ryan's every thought, feeling and emotion yet unuttered. Ryan now hears joy and gladness and is satisfied. Ryan has discerned healing for his ears, turmoil and anguish have ceased. Peace reigns. Ryan was searching for God and as a young boy accepted Him. To everything there is a season and a purpose under heaven. Death is a conquered foe. Jesus is the good Shepherd Who knows and recognizes His own and Ryan knows and recognizes Him. God gave His very life and laid it down for all of humanity. The constraints and limitations of Ryan's earthly shell were too confining and he could no longer see the beauty of the world, but his sadness is now turned to joy and he knows the truth in his inmost heart. I*

believe that God has raised Ryan to a heavenly dignity and he has clarity of mind
without mental illness because now he has the mind of Christ.

2001
Mother's Journal

We must flesh out our beliefs. God appoints time and it is in His hands. One day there will be an end to time, but it is not yet. (Daniel 11:27) I have to figure out the best way to live. God has taken full responsibility for my life since the day I gave my heart to Him. Because of His blood and the Cross my future is secure, my inheritance guaranteed, and my destiny certain. Jesus would never ask me to do something without His grace. In darkness, He's my light; in trouble, He's my security; in uncertainty, He's my guidance; and in fearful times, He's my peace. I will never face a day without Him; I will never take a step without His presence walking beside me; never face a need without His supply; and never face a circumstance He can't bring me through.

I wrote that journal entry five years before Ryan died. Was God speaking to my heart, even then, preparing me for the early death of my son? I admit powerlessness to have affected a change. My prayer was that my children would hit the mark that God set for them. I Corinthians 13 says, "Love's hopes are fadeless under all circumstances and it endures everything without weakening. For our knowledge and our teaching are fragmentary but when the Complete and Perfect comes the imperfect will pass away." It is You, Lord who gives me the power to do hard things.

William Blake said, "Life's dim window of the soul distorts from pole to pole, and leads you to believe a lie, when you see with, not through the eye." I must learn to see *through* the eye. I must learn to put my eyes back on Jesus, Who, for the joy of obtaining the prize that was set before Him endured the cross, despising and ignoring the shame. How Jesus endured the pain of the present was to fix His eyes on the prize of pleasing the Father and with patience, endured.

Ryan must have felt such hopelessness as the illness slowly clouded his judgment, but I don't believe it totally obliterated his emotional attachment to his family, the sadness just got in the way. Life can be unspeakably sad. When we do get a taste of what we really long for—it doesn't last. And then we feel guilty about our disappointment because we know we're made for so much more. God has set eternity in our hearts and will make everything beautiful in its time, said the writer of Ecclesiastes. He is Lord over every loss, every heartache. He is Lord of all comfort and mercy, resurrection, restoration, regeneration and of life.

Hope is for the soul what breathing is for the living organism. C.S. Lewis said in *The Weight of Glory*, "The door on which we have been knocking all our lives will be open at last."

Life is messy and often prevents us from seeing that what we needed has been with us all along. God was with Ryan in the midst of his dark suffering, even though he didn't get the relief he sought. He was with me through my mistakes, my wanderings, and in the agony of this earthly separation.

It is through struggle that we reveal to the world where our treasure lies. My treasure is not of this world, but the one to come. I want to make people's opinion of God better because of my life, because of Ryan's life, in the hope that they will continue knocking on that door.

I thank writers C.S.Lewis, John Eldredge, John and Frances Gunther, Viktor Frankl, Blaise Pascal, Joan Didion and Annie Dillard, for all have helped me find my way in the dark. There is no neat and tidy package called *resolution,* and some days I still feel lost in my own life. But if I listen carefully I can hear the faintest of whispers, "I know where you are."

So, what difference does faith make? It makes all the difference between despair and hope, death and life. God invites us to gaze upon the image of the crucified in order to soften our hearts towards Him, to still believe in His goodness, and to realize that, as Christians, our suffering has meaning. He gathers our tears, calms our sorrows and points us towards His resurrection. Time upon this earth is a mere moment when compared to eternity. I still believe.

"A Mother Gives Birth"

A mother gives birth, but she is not the life giver.
It is God Who holds the seed of spirit and blows the breath of life into formless flesh and blood.
A mother, taking her God-given role, partners with the Creator to love the child unconditionally.
She allows her soul to mingle with the life that came forth from her body, thus cementing the bond for all eternity.
But, in doing so, she opens her heart to the inevitable pain of the child's life . . .

As he grows, spreads his wings, falls, and tries again,
She holds his precious dreams within her soul and prays that he
will flourish and become all God created him to be.
Miracle of divine proportions—a life she did not create, but for
whom she would die.

Glory of glories, "Can a mother forget the child at her breast?"
Symbolic of Christ's love as He descended into hell and suffered so
we would know God and receive eternal life. This love cannot fail.
But a mother is only human after all, imperfect as any other human
being.
A mother cannot save her child from mental illness.
A mother's love cannot protect from the pain and tedium of the
child's daily struggle for normalcy.
Nor can her love save from death. Only the Savior can.

An ambivalent ache radiated through her as she struggled to care
for the child whose illness became overwhelming. He had no peace,
and she was barely surviving herself.
Where were her powers of problem solving, where were her advocacy
skills when the specter of mental illness came to live at her house?
She was paralyzed. The numbness allowed her to face the long days
of her child's despair.

She hoped and trusted in his words that he would never kill himself.
But it happened. It wasn't his wish to die–it was the illness.
So what do mothers do when they've done their best but it's not
good enough?
To Whom do they turn?
"I look to the hills from whence cometh my help. My help comes
from the Lord."
The mother must be gentle with herself. She must see herself
through God's eyes; carved in the palm of His hand, just as she saw
the child that God had lent her.

A mother gives birth, but she is not the life giver. Death has come.
All the days of the child's life were written in God's book before
they took shape, when as yet there were none.

Reach out through the darkness of death, the unknown unanswerable why and cling to the deep abiding love He placed in the mother's heart, the love that cared for the child during his season on earth. Once again, at the appointed time she will see the child of her womb. Look forward with hope; knowing the child is safely Home.
Desiree Woodland ©2006

Chapter Nine

CONTINUING BONDS

Ryan was not the illness. I am reaching for a positive bond with him, but the idea of letting go of the sadness of his final years has been torturous. When someone you love dies from a heart attack or cancer, you remember him in relation to his life. This is not true of suicide. The sad details mixed with guilt threaten to strangle survivors. To let go of the most powerful bond which has been the pain, and exchange it for a clearer, more comforting inner representation of his new life is healing, but also elusive. For many long months after he died I could only see the years of his suffering and the worst last months of his life. But, rather than identifying so strongly with Ryan's pain and the magnitude of his death, I am learning to make a conscious choice, maybe over and over, to identify with the energy and love that was in the living child.

Our task is to learn to live with this permanent change in our lives, not to get over a temporary disruption. The bond we are rebuilding with Ryan must somehow represent both his presence and his absence. If not for the love of God expressed in Jesus Christ I am not certain we could do the hard work of moving through the pain to the place where we will be healed as much as is possible this side of heaven.

Early in my grief I wrote about creating this new bond with him. I think I knew even then that the old bonds that had held us together would no longer work and new ones would have to be forged.

I love you with a growing sense of your new place in my life.

Ryan was the son we needed in our family. He was the last to join us, and even though he was the first to leave, we are eternally grateful that he came. His quiet demeanor calmed us and he seasoned our lives with grace. He enjoyed a good argument, but when the dust settled he still managed to be a peacemaker and show it by his actions.

Ryan's Journal

"Please don't remember the Ryan of the past five years. Remember the fun-loving, carefree Ryan. Please"

I will try, Ryan. I will write what I want always to remember: The good years of Ryan's life, the wonderful family times, the life he lived with pure joy and gladness.

One such memory is when, at age ten, Ryan gave up his private plans for how to spend his summer vacation. A neighbor needed childcare for her two children, and despite being close to his age, Ryan thought it might be hard to spend the entire summer with kids who liked different things. I heard the worry in his voice. He had already made some specific plans for summer, he wanted to explore the acequia to hunt for crawdads and ride his motorcycle around the ditches near our home.

After a quick family meeting we reached the conclusion that our neighbors needed our help and it wouldn't hurt too much to change some of our plans. Following some initial whining and complaining he made the best of it. He exchanged his vision of lazy summer days for another kind of adventure. Wanting to learn how to build something, the idea of a fort popped into his head. Ryan asked Dad for the 'how to' and then gathered his supplies: wood, nails, old carpet and other cast off materials. Tools in hand, all three friends began to work with gusto on the following day. Sounds of sawing and hammering filled the air along with the joyful laughter of kids doing real work. The end result was a clubhouse of sorts complete with windows and a roof! I cherish a faded picture taken on the day they dedicated the clubhouse. All three of them are standing beside a sign that reads, *No Girls Allowed,* smiling triumphant smiles. I think it was one of the best summers of Ryan's life.

Closer to the years before he left, I desperately tried to get him back into life. Ryan used to love the out of doors so when I suggested a hike at the base of the Sandia Mountains, he agreed. The mountains were lit that morning with a purple hue as the sun slowly crept over the horizon. The wildflowers seemed to wave at us with joy. Riding in our old Jeep, we pulled up to the trailhead and he slammed on the brakes. The tires screeched and gravel went flying through the air. He looked over at me and began laughing his infectious laugh. He enjoyed making me nervous, but instead of protesting, I started laughing too. I don't know if he knew, but I always felt safe with him.

On this day he seemed easily content to spend time with me and the expectation of a beautiful morning hike lay before us like an unwrapped gift. Ryan had organized supplies, packed our lunch, filled bottles with water, and the Jeep with gas. "Did you remember the sunscreen?" I asked before he locked the car. Nodding, he slung the backpack over his shoulder and we started out. Chamisa and scrub lined the sandy trail, the bees buzzed lazily around us, and we were happy. No worries, no deadlines, just a sunny day spent enjoying nature and being together. I drink in this memory and it fills me. I am honored that he spent time with me on that summer day. I think it was easier for him than being with his friends.

Ryan's family still needs him, but he is not here. The grief is unspeakable at times, the permanence of missing him, the letting go that can only come in degrees, the sadness we feel as his face seems to fade, not in our heart, but in our mind's eye. The time for building new memories has past.

I will always cherish his life and his death, and hold them tightly within my heart, even while I strain to press forward into life. Writing is a tool to process the emotions, thoughts, and experiences of this kind of pain, and without it I could not press forward. Nor would I be able to remember the important things about him. Without writing I would be unable to come to terms with the magnitude of this loss.

> *It's surprising how much of memory is built around things*
> *that are unnoticed at the time.*
> Barbara Kingsolver

God forbid that we should not remember the past, the good times, the hard times, the successes and mistakes. But, death has come. Our relationship is no longer emotional or physical but rather historical. Is it not possible that the work of memory provides spiritual threads that keep us connected with our loved one?

At one time Ryan described himself as strong, stable, decent and patient. I wanted to remember him this way, rather than just in the ways the illness had changed him. That was the challenge.

I worked to distill my grief into foundational beliefs, unable to move into the future unless the foundation was rebuilt. True faith is an invitation to trust in the promises of God, wherever that leads. These words became a tribute and statement of those foundational beliefs, inspired by Joyce Sackett's memoir about her daughter's suicide, called *Goodbye Jeanine*:

> "When Ryan entered the home of God it was also the home of his true self. There is no more false self in him. He came home to himself in wholeness, goodness and the fullness of beauty. He knows clearly and completely that he is truly made in the image of God. In heaven Ryan's true essence is unencumbered by sin. His parents will take full pleasure in his creative and healthy mind, which has plumbed the depths of the mysteries of life. We will know as we are known, we will see and understand our own beauty and the glorious beauty of everyone else."

> *Although death is never a beautiful thing, we have to die first in order to live. In Ryan's eyes he had to die so he could live. The fact that he could not gain the victory he desired on this side of heaven makes him no less a victor in God's eyes! And what one man sees as failure, God only sees as victory through the cross.*
> Barbara Kimberly

Perhaps I can say that Ryan chose to enter his Father's house before his place was ready. But our Lord who numbered the hairs on Ryan's head, and bought him with a price, calling him by name, will not turn him away. As a good host faced with an unexpected guest, he hastily makes the preparations with pain in his heart for the manner in which he came, and for the agony of his parents and friends, but with an ocean of love for him.

Ryan is completely complete and perfectly perfect. Every tear, fear and regret has been washed away—free at last. Free to play his music and to be in a band. Free to use the brilliant mind God gave him, to know the mysteries of the universe, and to know God. On earth he was bound by human limitations. I look forward to the day I will look into his eyes and know what he already knows.

"How Many Ways Do I Remember?"

I love being your mom, my precious boy.
I loved the dignified respect you showed for your family and friends.

I loved your handsome face, your strength, and willingness to help others.

I loved how you always said, "Goodnight" and "I love you, Mom."

I loved the pride on your face the first time you rode your bicycle.

I loved your quick mind—always thinking out how or why things worked,

I loved your skateboarding grunge days.

I loved the swagger you developed to keep your size 38 pants up!

I loved the letters and love notes you left me to find during your elementary years.

I love remembering the sweetness of your having been on the earth: happy days, music, cars, and stereos.

I love that you were a seeker. You endeavored to be all you could be, and in spite of the limits your mind placed upon you, you cared about learning.

I remember discussions of world issues and philosophy. Albert Einstein said, "Religion without science is lame, but science without religion is blind." You agreed.

There is an element to humanity that is mysterious. Yes, Ryan you knew and you know.

I love the memory of driving to the gas station each Sunday to wash our cars. Your black Integra was your pride and joy. It became too loud for your ears and you sold it, but always wanted to replace it. I hope you are now driving one restored exactly as you dreamed!

I love your tenacity in holding on to this life, for our sakes, even when you suffered to do so.

I love that you spent your last day on earth with me-despite the terror of knowing it might be your last. You gave me the gift of being with you.

Desiree Woodland ©2006

It is ironic that the illness that took Ryan's life was strongly connected to his hearing, since it was music that he loved. Music and conversation. Even when it became increasingly difficult to be around people, he always tried to listen to his friends. In spite of his inability to have continued these friendships over the years, the friends remained loyal. They told me that Ryan was someone who listened from his heart. *Ryan, your friends knew that you really cared. Your friends loved you and they love you still.* These are the kinds of positive bonds that will continue to be strengthened by the constant and consistent love of Ryan's friends and family.

"Eternity"

I struggle against the barrier,
pushing and straining to break free from the limits of time,
trying to regain the relationship I once shared with my son.
All the while knowing it is futile to try,
for it will never again be on this earthly terrain.
I must release him from the limits of earth and embrace him in the spirit.
With the eye of faith I see his handsome face now filled with inexpressible joy!
He's safe now and surprised to be loved.
The thin veil of separation does not permit us to be together yet,
but I can reach out in faith to our Creator and allow Him to connect us.
Son of my youth, whom I am learning to set free from my earthly,
grasping, clinging, and often doubt-filled heart.
In setting Ryan free, I am set free.

Desiree Woodland ©2006

Chapter Ten

WHAT I KNOW FOR SURE

Grieving is not just something that we do on sad occasions. It is a mode of existence that agrees to carry the sadness of things without denying or dismissing the pain as an accident. It is a way of living that incorporates dying. It is a way of remembrance that refuses to forget. It is not a maudlin, depressed or self-pitying thing, but a way of "compassion" that makes room for everything and holds onto nothing. Tears stream down the cheek to make room for more inside the eye. Richard Rohr

Experts say that each person grieves in their own way, at their own pace. People who don't understand can hurt the newly bereft with words like *it's taking so long* or *your loved one is in a better place,* or *surely you are over it by now.* It is hard to see sadness on someone's face as they struggle with fresh grief and the early learning of how to deal with their child's death. It will take patience and understanding on the part of friends, because in this school of learning there is no graduation.

Each friend and family member, who pushed past their own aversion to sadness and allowed us to speak about Ryan, shared our burden and became a blessing. For the bereaved to hear the name of their loved one does not increase melancholy, in fact it often has the opposite effect and releases the sorrow that builds up from time to time.

Amazing love was displayed to us and became a reminder of God's love, a reminder we desperately needed. It gently touched us in spite of the anger, questions and disappointment we felt with God. Our lives were embellished with the love and care of others who allowed us to lean on their faith when we said *we still believe, but Lord help our unbelief.*

The morning after Ryan died, there on my doorstep, was a friend who didn't wait to see if she could help, she just came. She came with her faith that God was surely in control, even if we couldn't sense His presence. She came with hot coffee and scones. She came with her arms full of necessities; a journal to record memories, Kleenex for crying and a list of people to bring meals. Carol made phone calls, helped with arrangements, and answered the phone because she knew we couldn't. The love of God flowed through her heart to ours. Somehow she knew that words were too narrow to adequately describe the immensity of all that had happened, and so she and her family just sat with us in our grief. Their kindness extended into the weeks and months following Ryan's death. And as gently as they came, she and her husband Dana, gradually faded from our lives back into their own. But they left a mark in our hearts that will never be forgotten.

Each day for several months when I opened the mail box I found it filled with sympathy cards. Some people had been touched with the loss of a child too, but each card was a personal expression of love in the midst of our loss. They became sacred witnesses and reached out to love us in our pain.

Society gives people such little time to grieve. The average bereavement leave from employment is five days. Five days to process the loss of someone we love. Impossible! Active grieving is a long process that demands our full attention for a while.

The principal of the school where I worked gave permission to take off as much time as I needed. I couldn't imagine ever returning, but was thankful not to feel any additional pressure. Once again, I was given a strand of grace and the room to breathe in my sorrow.

I did not return to teaching that year. Ryan's death occurred one month before summer break, so a long-term sub was hired. I felt I had abandoned my students without explanation. On one Friday I was their teacher and the next Monday I wasn't. I owed my students more than that. I wanted them to know I loved them, and even though I wouldn't be coming back to finish the year, they were important. Even more, I hoped that by listening to *Tear Soup,* they would learn a powerful lesson about death—that even when death touches us in the most horrific manner, we honor our loved ones by learning how to grieve openly. The students didn't know the manner of Ryan's death, only that their teacher was sad and wasn't coming back.

The gym was filled with sixth grade students along with the social worker, the principal, and other staff members, as well as a friend whose heart had told her I needed support. She stood behind me as I talked with my students and her presence was a comfort. I spoke simple words of explanation about losing Ryan. I told them I wanted to read *Tear Soup* because it described what the process of grief was like, since I had no words of my own yet. I explained that the story tells how Grandy went about cooking a big batch of tear soup because someone important in her life had died. Soup making became her metaphor for the grieving process. There was a respectful silence throughout the room, and I felt myself slowly leave my body, and I watched myself perform this unimaginably hard task from another vantage point. I heard myself reading purposefully, not stumbling over or choking on words. It was if God was directing me in this scene of my life. I read it all the way through even though my heart was breaking. When I finished and closed the book, I looked out over my students, who by now had risen to their feet, tears streaming down some of their faces. "We love you Mrs. Woodland." *I love you too*. Some of them waited in line to share hugs, and poetry that they had written. It was an unforgettable experience and I am ever grateful that I pushed through my discomfort to receive this tangible grace for my journey.

Another tangible grace came through the financial support we received. We were already overcome by the spiritual and emotional demands of death, but monetary costs could have added an extra burden. Living in the fog of fresh grief, we were ignorant of the high cost of dying. But God knew, for He used the people in our lives. Collections taken at my school and Gary's work paid for Ryan's funeral. And Ryan left his own instructions, "Sell my car and tools. This should help with funeral expenses." We had no plan in place or directions to follow on how to go about burying our child, for children are not supposed to die first.

As time passes, it will always be important to know that the memories of loved ones live in the hearts of others. My sisters, Sondra, Jocelyn and Jeannine, and Ryan's cousin, Missy never mind sitting with me while I make a fresh batch of tear soup. They listen with their hearts, even as their eyes well with tears. We believe in God and yet we cry. When I yearn for Ryan's physical presence, through their emotional presence, I receive comfort.

Love goes very far beyond the physical person of the beloved.
It finds its deepest meaning in his spiritual being, his inner self.

The prayers, the encouragement, the love, and the mementos we received have eternal meaning and helped us search for the deepest meaning in Ryan's death. Meaning that comes not just from the physical world, but the spiritual as well. It was and is spiritual work, to gently walk alongside us as we make our way through uncharted territory. Even though no one can share the pain—it truly belongs to me alone, Gary alone, and Michelle alone, but the encouragement and love are our inspiration to keep on trying.

How broadly God has spread this safety net in our lives. Each person is a link with our future—albeit a different future than we had planned. And each played a part in helping us give Ryan back to God, sometimes many times in one day. This letter expresses the depth of our feelings:

Dear Friends,

Life contains many mysteries . . . some pleasant, some unpleasant. The human struggle on this earth has purpose if only we look at our circumstances through God's love rather than looking at God's love through our circumstances. The horror of this earthly separation from Ryan is tempered with our faith that it is only a temporary separation. He is with God and we will meet again. God in His wisdom has allowed us to only see through a glass darkly walking through the mystery and wonder of this life. Our existence on the planet is for the glory of God. We could not come to the place of submission to His Lordship unless we see the need to. Without pain we would not even be able to comprehend the beauty in the world, or the glorious work of Christ for our salvation both here and forever. Pain and suffering are the price for a free will. We can choose to submit to the Creator or not.

We come to Him with broken hearts. He meets us with the balm of healing covering us with His grace. We are His instruments in this life. He uses people to bind up the brokenhearted and to mourn with those who mourn. We have found much comfort and grace to endure and indeed to survive because of your hands extended to us. God has conquered death and the grave; and eternity has been on my mind since Ryan's death. This world is only a drop of time into eternity, but it has seemed endless for us at times.

To say that God is good and His plan is perfect is something each human being struggles to reconcile. Humanists like Bertrand Russell scoff, "What kind of a god would allow suffering of this magnitude and be God?" I have felt the bitterness of those words upon my own tongue and the darkness of unbelief. God cannot be proven or disproven scientifically, so what kind of answer will satisfy? How will I respond in a way that allows me to "keep on keeping on?" From deep within my broken heart come these words: A God Who is sovereign over the earth that He created, but the earth through sin has fallen, is subject to decay and is pierced with sorrow . . . . all to give us the opportunity to make a free choice whether to serve him or not.

The law of the universe is a cycle of life, death, and regeneration. Move with the rhythm of the Creator, not fearing when pain and sorrow come. We believe that Jesus was in the depths of Ryan's suffering with him, Ryan was never alone. Why wasn't he healed? We prayed daily for a release. His release did come, but not in a way we would have chosen. God in His mercy said to Ryan, "You have come to journey's end." We believe (knowing what we know about mental illness) that Ryan was spared even greater torment in the future. Too many ill people wander the streets homeless—never being free—Ryan was in such torment. He called out to God—but couldn't find Him—He called out to God's mercy before he died and we know God's grace and mercy flooded his heart and mind with the Light of eternity. He is free, he is free, he is free! Jesus came to lead Ryan out of this prison and restore his soul. He is a soaring spirit alive to God. God's healing is completely complete and perfectly perfect.

"Yearning for God is the hunger that most often goes unrecognized in our lives. Other hungers are satisfied, sometimes on an epic scale, but they are not enough." I ponder this quote found yellowed on a scrap of paper in the back of my Bible. This yearning is created when our lives come crashing in upon us. Hope is as reasonable as despair when facing the unknown.

Pain is inseparable from love: that is a truth we must live with. It is a proof of our true inner reality, and a judgment of us as to how and with what courage we face and accept that truth.

Please know that your love and faith are invaluable to us. We are eternally grateful for all you mean to us and for all you have done for us. None of us could ever make this journey alone. We thank you also on behalf of Ryan who is blessed to know his parents have such support through the grace and love of the Father.

Sometimes days get easier, and then a wave of grief and sorrow come and I can do nothing but weep. I miss him and long to see him again. The pain knocks me over. Gary and I have realized how sick his mind was and how he suffered the black night of depression that wouldn't let him see beauty in the world anymore. He suffered from a delusion that wouldn't let him recognize that he wasn't going deaf . . . that it was still possible to still his anxious thoughts with the music that he loved so much. He only knew the utter turmoil of the day and night terrors. How hard it is to let go of these things. We know that we must go on in hope of the future for Ryan's sake. We continue to ask for your prayers that we will know and see color in our world once again, in spite of the sorrow that will always be a part of life on this earth. Love, Gary and Desiree

In spite of the difficulty of naming the feelings that assaulted us in those horrible months and years following Ryan's death, Gary and I walked together. Sometimes silence became the words, but in that silent sorrow, woven throughout our beings, our hearts beat as one. The death of a child can sometimes rip at the fabric of what brought two people together, and irreparably damage the expectations that life once held to continue on as a family. But again without words, we sensed that there was no blame to assign, no fault to cite in the other, only a knowing that we would not let the loss of our son tear apart the relationship we had built together before God. Although Gary does not and will not express his grief in the same ways I do, I know without any doubt that God has sustained his faith, albeit changed as it is, through His mercy and loving kindness. That same mercy and loving kindness has sustained, and will continue to sustain our relationship with each other.

Yes, our family constellation has changed. For holidays, birthdays, and vacations there will always be an ache for the loss of Ryan's physical presence. At a Survivors of Suicide meeting someone said that out of death there would come forth gifts. A painful idea when one is in the depths of fresh grief. But with a heart full of grace we sense that nothing is wasted. All can be used for God's glory.

"Homesick"

When I get Home, I will see what God meant when He created Ryan
His brilliant thinking and gifted creative spirit
Ryan, in the fullness of joy
and fullness of who God created him to be.
As a young boy Ryan asked Jesus
into his heart, and Jesus never moved out.
I am homesick knowing that my son is waiting.

Desiree Woodland ©2006

Chapter Eleven

EPILOGUE

Acceptance

Stop chasing the person you once were.
Who you are now and what you will become in the future
is tentative and uncertain.

Unpeeling the layers of this unnatural loss means grief upon grief. The loss of a child before the parent, the intractable illness and the added burden of death by suicide, has weighed upon me heavily. Becoming a survivor of Ryan's suicide is work I am ill-prepared to do, and yet there is no other way but through. There have been many threads of grace, but the shock and pain were so intense I couldn't recognize them all. I have been humbled by true friendship framed by love, the rebuilding of a surety of hope in God and acceptance of the mystery for which we, along with the rest of creation, wait to be revealed.

It's the Heart That Matters More—in this title from Counting Crows, a music group that Ryan liked when he still listened to music, I see a metaphor for mental illness. If the illness takes our loved one away and they retreat into a place in their own minds where no person or medication can reach them, it's still the heart that matters more. Just as God looked on David's heart . . . He looked on Ryan's. In the Old Testament when the people desired a king, the Lord said to Samuel, speaking of David, "For the Lord sees not as man sees, for man looks on the outward appearance, but the Lord looks on the heart." I Samuel 16:7.

Grief too, is heart work, and we accept that it takes as long as necessary and that it may never be completely finished. As the years pass and I move into the future, I am learning to be comfortable with my own needs, not ignoring the labor pains as I birth this life without Ryan. I seek to be sensitive to its contractions, not burying them underneath the busy-ness of life. On some days the grief is most noticeable, on others the happy memories shine through, but every day I am cradled by the conscious hope of being reunited with him.

Acceptance can only come, when we realize that a stage in our lives has ended. If we stubbornly cling to what we once had, we will lose the impact and meaning that surely awaits us. We risk limping through our days, never at peace, never fully present for those who remain. How is it possible to arrive at this place called acceptance? Acceptance is bitter and can only be digested bit by bit, hour by hour, day by day, as we reflect on what we believe. We don't allow the busy-ness of life to crowd out the import of what has happened. Life is different now. We are different now. As survivors of suicide, I don't think we will ever arrive at a point where we say, "Now it's all over."

It is as if I must absorb it, allow myself to be filled with it, feel it, and even embrace it until the burden becomes too much to humanly bear. I push this pain away, but in order to live well I must integrate Ryan's illness, as well as his death, into my life. Living well; the very words get stuck on my tongue.

How am I now to live? Yes, more deeply, more consciously, and more present than before. But, if I am ever to live with gratitude for life again, I cannot be afraid of the gnawing ache that still comes at times unbidden. Being thankful means I am infinitely more grateful that Ryan was here and graced my life, believing the pain of his departure is worth it, rather than never having known him. Survivors make a determination that somehow our lives *will* make a difference.

And being convinced of God's sovereignty, I say with Paul, "I am persuaded, beyond doubt, am sure . . . that nothing can separate us from the love of God in Christ Jesus our Lord." Romans 8:38. I lean into the thought that God is God and I am not. And since I believe that He is good, I hope in time to see the good that He has wrought through the awfulness of Ryan's illness and death. Words from ancient Hebrew believers soothes the ache in my heart, "Each one of these people of faith died not yet having in hand what was promised, but still believing. . . . By seeing it off in the distance, waved their greeting and accepted the fact that they were transients in this world. People who live this way make it plain that they are looking for their true home." (Hebrews 11:13-16). Reminders of it are everywhere, if I am open to see. In many ways, this book will never be finished because I am unfinished.

"My Life is in Pieces"

My life is in pieces, mere fragments and memories,
Images and feelings
Lying scattered on the floor and I frantically try
To recreate my life from those jagged remnants.
Grief does that.
It shreds the whole into parts of unrecognizable sizes, shapes and patterns.
How will my life ever be pieced back together?
Will it still be a thing of beauty to God after I have torn
and frayed the edges of each dark shape?
Will they ever mingle with other colors, lighter and more like my old life?
I desperately try to still the storm inside my heart.
Lord, you must keep the seams together before I come apart.
Direct the needle and thread, stitch the pattern you think best
Cut loose the threads that bind my heart to this fragile world,
Let me become what you desire.

Desiree Woodland©2006

The permanence of Ryan's absence sinks into my days. I have come here kicking and screaming, and yet I am arriving. I did not want to come, O Lord, I did not want to come. The longing for Ryan flows over me many times each day. But it is no longer the entire day. The struggle inside for healing and the letting go of his suffering and death do battle with the fear that the vivid memories will fade away with time and leave me with only misery, which will cripple me emotionally. Once again, I lean into the pain, softening, facing or embracing it, trying not to ignore it or stuff it back inside, but dealing with the reality of this enormous loss. It takes grace to do this. No human being chooses sadness.

Living through Ryan's illness and suicide, I confronted a profound sense of my own limitations. Most survivors of suicide, particularly of a child, search for reasonable answers to overcome the guilt and sharp fingers of accusation, but there are none. It takes plain guts and hard work to face the heavy burden of guilt. I taste the bitterness on my tongue as I 'try on' acceptance. It doesn't mean I am all right with this new life without my loved one, but only that I am learning to accept his absence.

The ability of one human being to help another, to alleviate their suffering, or to predict or prevent their suicide shows us our imperfections in such a painful way. There is no typical victim. As families, we are after all, only human and do the best we can. Suicide has changed my family and we will carry certain aspects of it with us always. We will never be the people we once were. We are older, wiser and sadder, but with God's help we will become stronger and more compassionate. Perhaps we will be braver and move into the future with this hard-won courage knowing we have faced the worst and survived.

The way through the world is more difficult to find than the way beyond it.

Ryan's legacy is contained within the hard-won wisdom that we continue to learn through his death by the grace of God. The mystery of deep love on this side of heaven involves suffering, as if suffering were built into the nature of love. As Ryan's parents, we are filled with longing that he would know and receive these words that still linger in the depths of our hearts; *Ryan, we understand that you did not willingly or intentionally want to hurt yourself or us. The delusion was your reality. We empathize with your pain, and that now, at long last, you are finally healed and made whole.*

How do we go about creating a new purpose for our lives? Will beauty be revealed out of the ashes? I want to honor God, honor Ryan, finish my race and help people understand why Ryan could not finish his.

But, the daily tasks of life can feel overwhelming in grief, and this is a natural reaction. When we experience a root loss we lose our footing, and feel lost in our own lives. Finding our way back to belief in life means we find a way to become reinvested. At first, I could not imagine caring about anything again. After the initial period of the most intense grief, which lasted three years, I came to realize I could not live out my days without honoring my son, and to not go on living my life honoring God would be a slap in Ryan's face.

Survivors must find a way to memorialize their children. We are all given the same choices, whether to stay preoccupied with grief, guilt and frustration, or to use these emotions as a catalyst to accomplish something of worth and value again.

I desired a new calling which would connect me to Ryan, even if it was dangerously close to my heart. I felt a yearning to be with others in their grief, so when I read about a workshop for future grief and loss facilitators, I signed up, not knowing whether or not I was ready to do something that might possibly reopen my wounds. But, it also contained the very real possibility of more healing.

"No one's death is ordinary." This profoundly satisfying statement struck a chord in my heart. The workshop speaker began to share ways to hold a sacred space for people in mourning. The Children's Grief Center was filled with people willing to give up two Saturdays in a row to practice doing just that. That first Saturday I met a special group of people who may or may not have experienced grief yet . . . but they would and they were willing to push past the discomfort of listening to others talk about death and personal sorrow. Becoming a grief facilitator has provided one way to live out my faith and honor Ryan.

I also began to volunteer with an organization called Casas de Vida Nueva or Homes of New Life. Several weeks before he died Ryan performed physical labor in the out-of-doors exhausting his body, but releasing endorphins that brought him a momentary sense of well-being. His journals say, "I wish I had lived on a farm 100 years ago." He thought it would help him to combat the stress of trying to live out his life with the oppressive belief that he was going deaf.

Casas de Vida Nueva will be the first therapeutic farm community in the southwest for people with mental illness, offering a place to become stabilized and receive treatment while working in a farm setting. Ryan would have thrived in this environment, and even though it wasn't available for him it will make a difference for other people's children.

The mental health field is plagued by disparities in the availability of housing and access to services. The implications of untreated and unrecognized mental illness exact a cost from families and society. Scientists may never entirely cure it, but something can be done to help heal the ruptures it creates. The healing farm may have been a place where Ryan might have learned acceptance of the illness and received peace. But, when treatment is ineffective or interventions fail, Christian hope offers something that therapeutic hope cannot: the promise that the sufferer remains loved and cared for by God.

Ryan wasn't the stereotypical image of a mentally ill person, and it went unrecognized for so long. Our assumptions of what mental illness looks like and the kind of people who become afflicted with it must be called to question. It afflicts all classes, races and sexes, and all kinds of families—abusive as well as loving, dysfunctional as well as stable. It is my prayer that I have challenged the prejudice, insensitivity and ignorance about mental illness and suicide by sharing Ryan's story.

The birthing of this book has been the result of a difficult and tedious labor. But nothing real or good comes without struggle. Life and death are held tightly in my heart, even while I yield to the unfolding of who I am now.

Ryan's life was humble, decent and good, and he touched us with love and joy, as well as sorrow. His legacy is not fame or fortune, but a memorial to show forth God's faithfulness in the midst of suffering. I still believe.

Notes

Scripture quotations are taken from the Amplified Bible unless noted otherwise. Copyright@ 1954, 1958, 1962, 1964, 1965, 1987 by the Lockman Foundation. Used with permission.

Chapter One

1. Corrine Chilstrom quoting Edwin Schneidman in *Andrew, You Died Too Soon* from his work *Definition of Suicide* (New York: Wiley and Sons,1985)
2. Corrine Chilstrom, *Andrew, You Died Too Soon* (Minneapolis, MN: Augsburg Fortress, 1993)
3. Carla Fine, *No Time to Say Goodbye* (New York: Random House, 2000)

Chapter Two

1. Vincent van Gogh, letters to his brother, Theo, 1880-1884.
2. Pearl Buck quote, source unknown.

Chapter Four

1. Lori Schiller and Amanda Bennet, *The Quiet Room* (New York: Grand Central Publishing, (Warner Books) 1994)
2. Pamela Spiro Wagner and Carolyn Wagner, *Divided Minds* (New York: St. Martin's Press, 2006)
3. Richard Keefe and Phillip Harvey, *Understanding Schizophrenia* (New York: The Free Press 1994)
4. Nancy Andreason, *The Broken Brain* (New York: Harper & Row, 1984)

Chapter Five

1. Richard Keefe and Phillip Harvey, *Understanding Schizophrenia* (New York: The Free Press 1994)
2. Gungsadawn Kataikaru (a student at Bryn Mawr) from a research paper on mental illness (*www.serendip.brynmawe.edu*)
3. David A. Karp, *Burden of Sympathy* (Oxford University Press,2004)
4. Kay Redfield Jamison, *Night Falls Fast* (New York: Vintage Books, 1999)
5. Stewart D. Govig, *Souls Are Made of Endurance* (Louisville, KY:Westminster John Knox Press, 1994)
6. 6. Nancy Andreason, *The Broken Brain* (New York: Harper & Row, 1984)
7. *Schizophrenic*, (UCLA, 1990)
8. Scott M. Peck, *The Road Less Traveled* (New York: Simon &Schuster, 1978)

Chapter Six

1. Jain Sherrard, *Mother, Warrior, Pilgrim* (Kansas City, MO: Andrews McMeel Inc, 1980) pg. 123 "After Today" used by permission of the author.
2. Patricia Hiscock, "Polishing Memories" used by permission of the author.
3. Scott M. Peck, *The Road Less Traveled* (New York: Simon &Schuster, 1978)
4. Sue Monk Kidd, *Love's Hidden Blessings: God Can Touch Your Life When You Least Expect It* (Ann Arbor, Michigan: Vine Books, 1990)
5. Jain Sherrard, *Mother, Warrior, Pilgrim* (Kansas City, MO: Andrews McMeel Inc, 1980) pg. 112 "Only This" used by permission of the author.
6. Lillian Moore, "Sunset" source unknown.

Chapter Seven

1. Martha Whitmore Hickman, *Healing After Loss* (New York: Perennial, 1994)

2. Corrine Chilstrom, *Andrew, You Died Too Soon* (Minneapolis, MN: Augsburg Fortress, 1993)
3. Dietrich Bonheoffer, from a quote in Martha Whitmore Hickman's, *Healing After Loss* (New York: Perennial, 1994)

Chapter Eight

1. C.S. Lewis, *Case for Christianity* (New York: Simon and Schuster 1996)
2. John Eldredge and Brent Curtis, *The Sacred Romance* (Nashville, TN: Thomas Nelson,1997)
3. C.S. Lewis in *The Problem of Pain* (New York: Harper Collins, 2001)
4. John Gunther, *Death Be Not Proud* (New York: Harper Collins, 1971)
5. Viktor Frankl, *Man's Search For Meaning* (Boston MS: Beacon Press, 2006)
6. Joan Didion, *Year of Magical Thinking* (New York: Knopf, 2005)
7. Blaise Pascal, *Pensees* edited by Richard H. Popkin, *Pascal Selections* (New York: Macmillan, 1989)
8. Annie Dillard, *The Writing Life* (New York: Harper Perennial, 1990)
9. William Blake, source unknown.
10. C.S. Lewis, *The Weight of Glory* (New York: Harper Collins, 1989)

Chapter Nine

1. Joyce Sackett, *Goodbye Jeanine* (Colorado Springs, CO: NavPress, 2005)

Chapter Ten

1. Pat Schwiebert and Chuck DeKlyen, *Tear Soup* (Grief Watch: Portland, Oregon)

About the Author

Desiree Woodland and her husband Gary live in Albuquerque, New Mexico. Ryan will always live in their hearts, while their daughter and amazing son-in-law live in Portland, Oregon with two grand dogs. Retired after seventeen years of teaching, she continues to tutor students, provide support for her mother with Alzheimer's and is pursuing education in the grief and loss field. This is sacred work that honors Ryan. She also uses every opportunity to speak up about the stigma of mental illness and suicide, and supports the Albuquerque—NAMI and Survivors of Suicide groups. *www.desireewoodland.com*

Websites

National Alliance on Mental Illness—*www.nami.org*

Survivors of Suicide—*www.sos.org*

Mental Health Education—*www.mentalhealthamerica.net*

Additional Recommended Books

Kolf, June Cerza, *Standing in the Shadow: Help and Encouragement for Suicide Survivors* (Grand Rapids, MI:Baker Books, 2002)

Kreeft, Peter, *Love is Stronger Than Death* (San Fransisco:Ignatius Press,1992)

Rynearson, Dr. Edward K. *Retelling Violent Death* (Philadelphia, PA: Brunner-Routledge, 2001)

Sheehan Susan, *Is There No Place on Earth for Me?* (New York: Vintage Books, 1983)

Winerip, Michael *9 Highland Road: sane living for the mentally ill* (New York: Vintage Books, 1994)

Zimmerman Susan, *Writing to Heal the Soul* (New York: Three Rivers Press, 2002)

Edwards Brothers, Inc.
Thorofare, NJ USA
July 20, 2011